The

COMPLETE
NATURAL
GARDENER

Also by Donald W. Trotter, Ph.D.

Natural Gardening A–Z

Other Hay House Titles of Related Interest

Aura-Soma: Healing Through Color, Plant, and Crystal Energy,
by Irene Dalichow and Mike Booth

Healing with Herbs and Home Remedies A–Z,
by Hanna Kroeger

The Essential Flower Essence Handbook,
by Lila Devi

(The above titles are available at your local bookstore,
or may be ordered by calling Hay House at
760-431-7695 or 800-654-5126.)

Please visit the Hay House Website at:
www.hayhouse.com

The
COMPLETE
NATURAL
GARDENER

How to Create Your
Own Garden Paradise

DONALD W. TROTTER, Ph.D.

Hay House, Inc.
Carlsbad, California • Sydney, Australia

Copyright © 2000 by Donald W. Trotter

Published and distributed in the United States by:
Hay House, Inc., P.O. Box 5100, Carlsbad, CA 92018-5100
(800) 654-5126 • (800) 650-5115 (fax)

Editorial supervision: Jill Kramer • *Design:* Jenny Richards

    The intent of the author is only to offer information of a general nature. In the event you use any of the information in this book for yourself, which is your constitutional right, the author and the publisher assume no responsibility for your actions.

[CIP data available from the Library of Congress]

ISBN 1-56170-716-3

03 02 01 00   4 3 2 1
First Printing, March 2000

Printed in the United States of America

Contents

Foreword

BY LOUISE L. HAY

"Feed the soil, and God will take care of the rest."

My earliest childhood gardening memory is of going into the woods behind our home and gathering leaf mold from California oak trees. It was quite undisturbed land, and the leaf mold must have been eight to ten inches deep. My stepfather and I would bring it back home and spread this mulch over the vegetable garden. I remember that it smelled of damp, musky earth, and I was told that this mulch was the best food we could give the garden. It was my first lesson in feeding the earth. I learned that the earth would be able to feed the plants that would then feed us.

Gardening is a lifetime of discovery. Wonderful little surprises await us if we are open. I remember how delighted I was when I discovered that I could get more than one cutting from a broccoli plant. Broccoli and zucchini are my favorite vegetables. I used to cut the broccoli head and then discard the plant. Once when I was in a hurry, I left what I thought was a spent plant in the ground. Two weeks later, I passed by this plant and found several new small shoots of broccoli. This was the sweetest, tenderest (eat them right in the garden) broccoli I had ever tasted. Now a broccoli plant stays in my garden $^2/_3$ months after the first cutting as I harvest $^7/_8$ more rounds of small but very delicious cuttings.

I am so blessed, because for years now I have been able to grow my own food. This is the ideal way to stay in tip-top health. In addition to armloads of flowers, I grow almost all my vegetables and many fruits. To pick fresh, ripe fruit from the tree or vine is a pleasure that is hard to surpass. When my Black Persian Mulberry tree gave me my first taste of its fruit, I was amazed by its sweetness. In the many years I had that tree, I could never get any fruit to the kitchen. I always stood under the tree, with juice dripping down my arms, eating as many ripe ones as I could find.

Being such a passionate, organic gardener myself, for many years I have wanted to share these ideas with all of you. However, writing a gardening book is not my forte. So for several years now, I have been looking for the perfect person to write such a book for Hay House. When I discovered Donald Trotter, I was ecstatic. Here was a man as passionate about gardening as I am, and with an encyclopedic amount of knowledge and a great sense of humor. It took awhile to persuade him to take time out of his extremely busy schedule to write this book. It was mostly written on airplanes as he dashed around the globe doing large projects such as moving trees from one country to another, or participating in large land-reclaim projects. Donald has helped many countries rebuild soil and bring their land back into high production. I admire him and the work he does immensely.

The precious time I have spent with Donald has given me great ideas for my own garden. It gets more beautiful and productive all the time. He knows of varieties of plants that I had not even heard of. Thanks to Donald, my roses are now absolute knock-outs—they seem to double in size and beauty and fragrance.

In the chapters that follow, you have an opportunity to learn to build soil in order to replenish the earth. This is what I have done for many years. Wherever I am, I rebuild the soil. Not a lettuce leaf nor a leaf from a tree leaves my property. Everything is ground up and returned to the soil. If I have a lot of space, I make a compost pile. If I have a little space, I grind up my kitchen waste with water in the blender and dig small holes in the garden and put it there. Either way I am always feeding the soil and the dear earthworms. In just one year, I can take a piece of barren hard soil (no earthworms), and by constantly feeding it organic matter, I will turn it into crumbly dark earth with an abundance of fat, happy earthworms. The tenant or landowner that comes after me always gets property that is more lush and abundant than the way I found it. When we give back to the soil, the earth/nature/God gives back to us abundantly. Every single thing I plant overgrows. It becomes bigger, fatter, and more productive than anything my chemical-using neighbor could possibly produce.

So we at Hay House offer this book to you with love, knowing that your gardening experiences will grow. You too will have the earth abundantly giving to you, much more than you have ever experienced before. Donald Trotter and I wish you happy gardening for the rest of your life.

Louise L. Hay

Acknowledgments

Gratefully . . .

There are some people who come into our lives who just need to be thanked—sometimes for no specific reason other than to show our gratitude to them for enriching our lives. My list includes my mom, Patsy, who gardens in the soil but cultivates a pretty good family as well. To my family—Clare, Patrick, Thomas, Michael, Dr. Auntie Ruth, Meghan, and Brandon—you are always in my heart. To Reid and Kristina, you guys are the best. To Scott and Shannon, thank you for your love and support. To Ava Frances, welcome to the world. I hope we will be able to give you the inheritance of a healthy place to grow up.

A special note to Louise: Passion is so essential to the quality of life. I have yet to meet someone as passionate about tending a garden. Your enthusiasm is a touchstone of hope for the future of this planet.

To the gang at Hay House: Thanks to Jacko and Tonya for your friendship and diligence in getting this reluctant writer out there to spread the word about gardening in partnership with nature. To Jill, I am amazed at your wordsmithing talents and will always be grateful for your patience. Christy and Jenny, your art is a reflection of the beauty we all aspire to in our lives. To Shelley, keep on singing! And to Ron, good gardeners always make the best people, and you are one of the best gardeners I know.

To the folks at Hearst: Rachel, thank you for bringing this California farm boy into The Big Apple. Kathryn, I will never be able to adequately express my thanks. Vicky, I thank you for the King's English and for your conversation and wisdom.

To Tiana: Thank you for your honesty, and I wish great fortune and complete fulfillment for you in your extraordinary life.

To the reader: A special thanks for opening this book. Whether you take it home or not, I hope you'll consider the fact that your personal space can affect all of us, and that minimizing your footprints of burden on the environment is something future generations of Earthlings will be grateful to you for. Enjoy this book, and I hope the information is useful, the humor is entertaining, and all of your gardens are alive with the gifts of nature. The Complete Natural Gardener *was written for you.*

At the time of this writing, we are all on the verge of entering a new century. My life is about to complete another trip around the sun, and we are cleaning up the environmental disasters our predecessors left us, paving the way for the passing of the smoke-spewing machine age and entering into the age of biology. As biotechnology improves, let's not lose sight of the biological diversity that created our existence in the first place. Let's consider the hybrid word Earthkeeper, *and try and use it when describing our own lives.*

Introduction

THE WAY
NATURE INTENDED

"Hello, fellow Earthlings!"

Welcome to *The Complete Natural Gardener.* This book is written for gardening enthusiasts of all skill levels for the purpose of making natural and organic gardening a quick and easy practice. In the following pages, I will be discussing topics that will assist you in achieving a greater understanding of how nature works, as well as allow you to tend to your garden without the need for synthetic chemicals of any kind.

Natural gardening is the practice of gardening organically and using only materials of natural origin to assist in cultivation. All aspects of a natural garden are friendly to the environment and actually promote a biological diversity that, as you will learn, actually helps to control pests and diseases, as well as improving soil and plant quality. The natural garden is a place where life abounds and is actively promoted in order to achieve lush, vigorous growth in any climate and in any soil. Guaranteed!

As you venture into this book, think of it as a walk in your own garden. It is written in a conversational tone that is intended to interact with you while you look at your garden spaces. The ideas, hints, and tips offered in these pages are all meant to help you increase your knowledge without resorting to a bunch of secret handshakes and confusing "gardenspeak." I would like you to imagine that I'm standing right next to you helping you dig away in your personal Eden— pulling weeds, pruning roses, and just chatting about the garden. While we take this walk together, our conversation will always be returning to the soil, where dirt is the primary topic. I like to think of this as the best way for perfect strangers to "talk dirty" to each other. Gardening is an exciting and fun hobby that is often tainted by dull and mundane language that is sometimes a little too scientific for casual hobbyists. We will be using none of that kind of talk in *your* garden!

You will hear several topics repeated throughout this book. The repetition is intentional, in order to express the importance of how natural gardening is an intertwined system that promotes and encourages plant growth by promoting and encouraging other life. It's strictly fun in the natural garden. If and when you choose to learn the language of gardenspeak, I suggest some horticulture classes at your local community college.

Once again, I welcome all of you who wish to garden naturally, and invite you to enter a place where environmental responsibility and the overall health of you and your family are priorities. In the natural garden, we will get to know each other while we learn how our planet supports and nurtures growth. We are about to embark on an amazing journey into the undersoil world of Dr. Don Trotter and a cast of billions of incredible organisms determined to make your garden a place of great beauty. So strap on those boots, put a coat on, and bring your book. This may take a while.

Let's go for a walk, and I'll see you in the Garden!

— *Don Trotter*

Chapter One

SOIL, THE GIVER OF LIFE

Most gardeners cultivate their gardens in *soil*. Soil is where nature decided her terrestrial masterpieces should grow. Soil is where the vast majority of our food supply comes from. And soil is what we live on. It is difficult to avoid our intimate relationship with soil and how connected the health of the soil is with our personal health.

What Is Soil?

Soil is a complex menagerie of minerals, organic matter, and life. It is different in its physical structure all over the world, and there can be several types of soil in an area the size of a parking lot. Soils are categorized into many different classifications that allow soil scientists and geologists to properly identify them. However, in this book, we will be focusing on four basic soil types: clay, silt, sand, and loam.

Clays are soils that have very fine particles and can be rather difficult to cultivate. This soil type is known for its ability to hold on to water. This water-holding capacity sometimes occurs to the detriment of plant growth. Clay soil particles can have a tendency to bind together and prevent essentials such as water and oxygen from penetrating where plants can use them. This is often one of the reasons gardeners have trouble cultivating gardens in clay soil conditions.

Watering clay soils and management of available water for plants is also a rather difficult proposition. Clay soils do not normally allow much water to enter and thus are considered to have a low rate of percolation, which is the vertical movement of water through soil. This is why many clay soils puddle water very quickly when irrigated or during rainy weather. This can cause problems with runoff and a potential loss of valuable nutrients that your plants require.

One of the easiest ways to determine if you have a clay soil is to walk on it when it is wet. If it takes your shoe off, chances are you have clay soils. Clay soils ball up in your hand when squeezed and do not crumble. One of the most common mistakes new gardeners make with clay soils is to believe that this type of growing medium will not grow a healthy garden. Clays are very good places to start. The addition of organic matter in the form of composts and mulches will begin a process of structural change in clay soils. By incorporating certain minerals into clay soils, you are also able to make clays open up to better water and air penetration. Clay soils hold on to moisture very well, and when they are properly amended with natural materials, they can support the growth of even the most demanding gardener.

Silt soils are much like clays, yet they have a little larger particle size. These soil types are very common and are widespread throughout areas where water once flowed. The fine particles of silty soils do have the same tendency to cling together that clay soil exhibits. Silt is less plastic than clay and will allow better water and air penetration, but it is also somewhat slow. Silty soils make excellent starting points for garden soil and respond quickly to the addition of copious amounts of organic matter in the form of composted manures, backyard composts, and organic mulches. Silts are often found in combination with clays, loams, and sandy soils. Soils with high silt content hold water very well and are capable of hanging on to nutrients longer than sandy soils. Silts also have the ability to take your shoes off when they're wet, so it's a good idea to wear boots or add a layer of mulch to them. Waiting for dry weather to retrieve one's footwear from the garden is not a pleasant aspect of the gardening hobby. Silty soil also balls up in your hand when squeezed, but it will crumble a little if it is not too wet.

Loams are considered the best kind of soil to grow plants in. This type of soil has a higher concentration of organic matter in it and is generally considered a very "fertile" soil type. Loamy soils have the best physical characteristics of the other soil types mentioned in this book. They will ball up when squeezed, like clays and silts, but crumble easily when the pressure of your hand is released. Loams often have a black or dark brown color, and you can see that the particles are much larger than those of either clays or silty soil types.

One of the primary ways to identify loamy soils is by smell. These soils have a rich, musty odor that just smells like it can grow anything you plant in it. I won't go too far into the taste of soils because you may not be inclined to eat your dirt in order to identify it. Loam soils contain *humus,* also. We will discuss humus in some detail later in this chapter, but suffice it to say that the presence of humus in loamy soils is a very good thing. These are the soils of the Great Plains of North America, and certainly the main reason why this has been considered to be one of the most significant regions for crop production in the entire world.

Sandy soils have a very large particle size compared to clays and silts. Because of this large particle size, air and water easily find space. This type of soil commonly percolates at a very high rate, and it is often a problem for gardeners because irrigation water or rainwater can pass right by thirsty roots. Obviously this is a problem that most folks with clay soils would love to have, but I think of sandy soils as the hardest ones in which to grow successful gardens unless heavy mulching is done to conserve moisture. Sandy soils also have a tendency to allow nutrients suspended in water to pass right through the root zone as well. This is one reason why folks who use water-soluble chemical plant foods have trouble in sandy soils keeping their plants fed.

Sandy soils can cause gardeners to give up trying to grow thirsty vegetables in favor of more drought-tolerant plant species. I say to you now that you need not give up on that patch of strawberries or those tomato plants, because all you need is mulch and compost. A natural gardener loves sandy soils because he or she can add organic matter to this soil type to assist in increased moisture retention and nutrient-holding capacity while enjoying the benefits of a well-draining soil. When sandy soils are amended with organic matter and mulched, they can support growth and hold sufficient water to sustain healthy gardens of any kind.

These few general examples of soil types will include your soil. As previously mentioned, there are countless combinations of these soils. There are sandy-loams, silty-clays, loamy-clays, and so on. Once you identify your basic soil type, you are prepared to make good decisions regarding soil amendments, fertilizers, and water management. Then we get to move on to the mineral characteristics of our garden soils. This includes *pH,* or the measurement of acidity and alkalinity.

The Secret of pH

As previously mentioned, pH is the way we measure how acidic or alkaline our garden soils are. The ways in which pH is measured are fairly simple and has been often overlooked as an important aspect of understanding the soil that our plants are growing in. Measurement of pH is no secret. It is, however, a somewhat unknown aspect of soil knowledge for many hobby gardeners. Hydrogen ion concentrations in a free state (not New Hampshire) are measured to calculate pH. Acidic soils have higher concentrations of free hydrogen ions than alkaline soils do. But here is the tricky part—the pH scale utilizes a negative exponent of the concentration. So, acidic soils are identified with a lower pH numeric value than alkaline soils. The pH scale goes from zero to 14, with zero being most acidic, and 14 being most alkaline. Neutral is defined as 7.0 to 7.2. Most plants prefer to live in soils between 6.5 and 7.5 on the pH scale.

The importance of pH is clear when we try to grow acid-loving plants in alkaline soils or vice versa. Gardeners in the Southwest want to be able to grow azaleas and gardenias, but they often have trouble due to incompatible pH values of their soils. This is a common problem, but without a basic knowledge of one's soils, countless innocent gardenia plants will give up the ghost because they can't live in their adopted home. When gardeners come into the nursery with that unfortunate plant, we are often given the cure to a smaller picture. If we first concentrated on the pH of the soil where we planted the deceased, we most likely would have found why it was sick before it croaked.

Testing the pH in our soils is a very basic process and does not require a degree in chemistry to perform or understand. We have the aquarium industry and tropical fish enthusiasts, as well as swimming pool products manufacturers to thank for easy-to-use and easy-to-read pH tests. The test kits that are available to most home gardeners utilize indicator materials that change colors when pH values reach a certain level. These tests are often liquid tests that require you to put some soil into a test tube and add the indicator and a little distilled water. They come with a color chart that you match up to the color of the liquid in the test tube to evaluate the pH of that particular soil sample. These pH kits are now widely available at many reputable nurseries and garden centers. They are also very inexpensive and can tell you more about your soil than any number of suicidal gardenia plants.

Now here's a bit of trivia. In 1909, a Danish chemist by the name of Soren Sorensen devised the pH scale to represent pH. The scale ranges from zero to 14, with zero to 6.9 indicating more acidic solutions (that is, those with higher concentrations of free hydrogen ions). Measurements of 7.5 to 14 indicate more alkaline solutions (those with lower concentrations of free hydrogen ions). The number 7.1 (pure water) represents a neutral solution. The *p* in pH is from the Danish word *potenz*, which means "strength"; the *H* is the chemical symbol for hydrogen. Thus, *pH* means "the strength of the hydrogen ions." Wasn't that fascinating?

The pH of soils can be altered quite easily for those of you hoping to actually grow that gardenia. There are a number of natural minerals that have the capacity to change soil pH in either direction. By applying particular minerals to your soil, you can make an acidic soil more alkaline or an alkaline soil more acidic. It is good to remember that a soil in the neutral range is capable of growing the widest selection of plant species. Let's talk about some of those minerals and how they affect plant growth as well.

Soil Minerals—Essential for Plant Health

This is the part of the book that gets a bit technical. I will do my best to explain the function of soil minerals to you by using everyday language, instead of resorting to a bunch of confusing words. Where terms are used that may be new to you, I will explain what they mean. Who knows, you may actually increase your vocabulary while learning some of the basic roles that minerals play in sustaining healthy plant growth.

Most soils consist of a complex mineral matrix where complicated electrochemical, biochemical, and biological activity determines every aspect of the soil's physical nature and its ability to support plant life. These minerals in combination with water and air consist of what is commonly called *the soil solution*. Plants are presently recognized to utilize 16 elements in order to sustain growth. Of these 16 elements, 12 are minerals found primarily in the soil. This is the part of this particular chapter where we could easily go into a litany of items on the periodic table of elements, but we'll stick to the basics.

Four elements that plants use are considered nonmineral and will be mentioned in detail later on. These elements are carbon, hydrogen, oxygen, and nitrogen. Carbon forms the skeleton of all organic molecules. Thus, it is a basic building block for all plant life. Plants take up carbon from the atmosphere in the form of carbon dioxide (CO_2). Through the process of photosynthesis, carbon is combined with hydrogen and oxygen to form carbohydrates. Further chemical combinations, some with the other essential minerals mentioned in this section, produce the numerous substances required for plant growth.

Oxygen is required for respiration in plant cells, whereby energy is derived from the breakdown of carbohydrates. Many of the compounds required for plant growth contain oxygen. Hydrogen combined with oxygen forms water (H_2O), which constitutes a large portion of the total weight of plants. Water is required for the transport of minerals and nutrients. It also enters into many of the chemical reactions necessary for plant growth while hydrating plant tissues. Hydrogen is also a constituent of many other compounds required for plant growth. These three elements are supplied to plants primarily from air and water. Plants that synthesize amino acids, which in turn form proteins, use nitrogen. Proteins are present in every living cell on the planet. Plants for other vital compounds such as chlorophyll, nucleic acids, and enzymes also require nitrogen.

The remaining elements known to be used by plants are found in mineral form and are primarily found in the soil. These minerals are phosphorus, potassium, calcium, magnesium, sulfur, zinc, iron, manganese, copper, boron, molybdenum, and chlorine. These minerals are commonly separated into three categories: primary, secondary, and trace. We will be focusing on these minerals in the order of the quantities that are used by plants in order to grow, along with their activity and effect on soil structure and fertility.

Phosphorus

Phosphorus is used by plants in different forms; availability of phosphorus to plants is dependent on the solubility of this mineral in soil. However, the availability of phosphorus is often tied up in compounds of limited solubility. The minerals that phosphorus links to depend on soil pH. In neutral to alkaline soils, phosphorus will link up to calcium. This forms a compound known as calcium phosphate, rendering the phosphorus unavailable to plants and making it insoluble. In soils with an acid pH, phosphorus will often link to iron or aluminum to form phosphate compounds that also bind phosphorus as insoluble and mostly unavailable to plants. These relatively insoluble forms of phosphorus are called *solid-phase phosphates* and can function as a phosphorus savings account in the soil. Isn't that clever? The amount of solid-phase phosphorus (phosphate) in a particular soil may actually account for 99% of the total phosphorus that appears in an analysis of the soil. This means that a little as 1% of the total phosphorus that shows up on a typical soil test may actually be readily available to plants.

Solubility of phosphorus is controlled by several factors, including the amount of solid-phase phosphorus present in the soil. The greater the total amounts present in the soil, the better the chance of having more phosphorus in solution. Another important factor is the extent of contact between solid-phase phosphate and the soil solution.

Greater exposure of solid-phase phosphate to the soil solution and to plant roots increases the ability to maintain replacement supplies. During periods of rapid plant growth, phosphorus in the soil solution may be replaced ten times or more per day from solid-phase phosphorus. Soil temperature and pH also affect the solubility of phosphorus. Maximum availability of soil phosphorus occurs at pH levels of 6.5 to 7.5.

Phosphorus is present in all living cells. It is used by plants to form nucleic acids such as DNA and RNA, and it is also utilized in the storage and transfer of energy through energy-rich linkages (ATP and ADP).

Some natural sources for phosphorus in the natural garden are soft-rock phosphate, hard-rock phosphate, and good old bone meal.

Phosphorus stimulates early growth and root formation in plants. It speeds up maturity and promotes flowering and seed production as well. Symptoms of phosphorus deficiency in plants include:

- slow growth; stunted plants;
- purplish coloration on the foliage of some plants;
- dark green coloration with the tips of leaves dying;
- delayed maturity; and
- poor fruit, flower, and seed production.

Potassium

Potassium is used by plants in the form of positively charged ions or "cations" (pronounced *CAT-eye-uns*). It is not synthesized into compounds the way phosphorus is, but tends to remain ionic within plant cells and tissues. Potassium is essential for the transport of sugars and for starch formation, as plants convert sunshine to food (photosynthesis). The pores in the leaves of plants (stomata) require the presence of potassium to open and close their guard cells in order to breathe. Potassium produces a higher function of vascular plant tissue for better transport of nutrients. It increases plant resistance to disease. It also increases the size and quality of fruits and vegetables.

Soils may contain 40,000 to 60,000 pounds of potassium per acre. However, only 1 or 2% of this amount may actually be available to plants in the soil solution. The rest is either tied up on particularly stingy clays known as expanding lattice clays, or it occurs in primary mineral forms that are unavailable to plants.

Supplemental potassium is often applied to natural gardens from powerful mineral sources such as potassium sulfate, which also adds some sulfur to soil. Other materials that supply potassium are kelp products, wood ash, an amazing material called *greensand,* and a mineral called *Sul-Po-Mag* (sulfate of potash magnesia). Sul-Po-Mag is a rich source of potassium, sulfur, and magnesium. Who says natural products can only do one thing at a time?

Potassium is used heavily by plants that have very high carbohydrate production rates, such as fruit trees. Potatoes use gobs of potassium due to their need to produce high levels of carbohydrates as starch in the potatoes themselves. Symptoms of potassium deficiency in plants include:

- tip and marginal (leaf edges) burn, starting on more mature foliage;
- weak stalks and stems;
- small fruit and shriveled seeds; and
- slow growth.

Calcium

Calcium is considered a secondary plant nutrient, but it is grossly underrated. It is the feeling of this natural gardener that calcium is just as important as nitrogen, phosphorus, and potassium for plant health and vigor. Calcium is absorbed by plants as a positively charged ion, or cation. It is an essential part of the structure of the cell wall in plants and must also be present in order for new cells to form. This means that if there is no available calcium, plants don't grow.

Calcium is used in acidic soils to raise pH values more toward neutral. The materials most often used to do this are *calcium carbonate* (lime), or calcium magnesium materials called *dolomite* and *dolomitic lime.* These materials supplement calcium to the soil for increased plant vigor, while they alter the pH in acidic soils. Calcium also affects clay soils by loosening the electrochemical bond between clay particles. This will allow for better water and air penetration into otherwise "tight" clay soils. In the western part of the country where soils are more alkaline, and in areas where little summer rain falls, a calcium and sulfur material called *gypsum* is often used. Gypsum does not alter soil pH nearly as much as lime products, and supplies an ample amount of calcium to increase plant health. Gypsum is also fairly effective at loosening clay and compacted silt soils that are often encountered on a newly constructed suburban lot.

In the last few years, a new material that supplies superior amounts of calcium has come to the attention of natural gardeners and farmers. This material is found in a fossil kelp (marine macroalgae) deposit that is actually located where an ancient ocean once was and what is presently called the state of Nevada in North America. This fossilized kelp material provides concentrated calcium and every other known plant growth nutrient, along with plant growth hormones as well. This material is known as *Kelzyme.*

A good thing to remember about calcium is that it is present in all living cells and is not mobile in plant tissue. What this means to a natural gardener is that composted plant matter is also a supply of calcium. So it is good to remember that a well-composted garden plot is also getting some calcium from that organic matter. Calcium deficiency is identified by some of these symptoms:

- Death of growing points (terminal buds) on plants
- Death of root tips
- Abnormal dark green appearance of foliage
- Premature shedding of blossoms and buds
- Weakened stems
- Blossom-end rot
- Crinkling of new growth

Magnesium

Magnesium is taken up by plants in the form of the positively charged magnesium cation. Cell division cannot take place without magnesium being present, and it serves as an activator for several plant enzymes required in the growth process. Magnesium is highly mobile in plants and can be moved from older to younger tissue rapidly in times of deficiency.

Magnesium can be supplied to plants from mineral sources such as dolomite lime, Epsom salts (magnesium sulfate), and Sul-Po-Mag (sulfate of potash magnesia). It is often applied to rose gardens to stimulate the growth of new canes. In western soils where rainfall is low, an abundance of magnesium can keep soils tight and impermeable to water penetration. The addition of calcium to soils high in magnesium will open them up to better water and air infiltration and improve percolation. The calcium magnesium dynamic in soils was studied and theorized by Professor William Allbrecht early in the 20th century. He theorized that five to seven parts calcium to one part magnesium improved plant growth and soil tilth, while enhancing plant uptake of other essential minerals present in soils.

Signs of a magnesium deficiency in plants often appear as:

- interveinal chlorosis (yellowing) in older leaves;
- upward curling of leaves along edges; and
- yellowing of leaf edges, with a dark green "Christmas tree" effect along the middle of the leaf.

Sulfur

The sulfur mineral is taken up by plants as negatively charged ions or anions (*AN-eye-uns*). Sulfur may also be taken up by plants from the air through the leaves in areas where industrial pollution from the burning of fossil fuels is enriched with sulfur compounds. Who says plants don't fight air pollution?

Certain amino acids that are essential for plant health (cysteine, cystine, and methionine) contain sulfur and are necessary for the synthesis of proteins. Sulfur is present in certain plant oils, which accounts for the odor of onions and garlic. It is also essential for nodule formation in certain types of plants that take nitrogen out of the atmosphere and fix it in the soil within the nodules. This group of nitrogen-fixing plants is known as the *legume* family and will be discussed later in this book. Sulfur is often applied to these plants to stimulate better nodule formation in order for legumes to fix more valuable nitrogen into the soil.

Sulfur is also known to suppress the growth of certain plant diseases and is often combined with calcium carbonate (lime) in commercial fungicides that natural gardeners find very useful.

Alkaline soils are often low in sulfur, so sulfur is applied to these soils to lower pH values and bring the pH more toward neutral. Sulfur is applied to soils in the form of soil sulfur, Sul-Po-Mag, iron sulfate, and other sulfate compounds. These are some signs of deficiency:

- Young leaves are light green or yellowish in color— in some plants, older tissue may also be affected.
- Plants are small and spindly.
- Interveinal chlorosis is found on plants or grasses.
- Plant growth is retarded, and maturity is delayed.

Iron

Ample amounts of iron are required for plants to make chlorophyll, which is the normally green pigment that is essential for photosynthesis. It is also an important activator of certain biochemical processes, such as respiration and symbiotic nitrogen fixation. Plants take up iron in the form of positively charged ferric or ferrous ions.

Iron availability is affected by soil pH, and when soils or alkaline iron is blocked. This is one of the reasons why iron chlorosis (interveinal yellowing) of foliage is so common in soils with a high pH. Lawns use a lot of iron and are often yellow due to a deficiency of this mineral. Gardeners often mistake an iron deficiency for a lack of nitrogen in their lawns and feed their lawns with high-nitrogen fertilizers that only green up their lawns temporarily. It is a good idea to identify when an iron deficiency is the cause of yellowing foliage. Checking the pH of your soil easily does this. If the pH is high and you fertilize regularly, chances are you can keep your lawn greener by adding an iron supplement to your soil instead of giving it another dose of nitrogen fertilizer. One thing to remember when applying iron to the garden is to keep it off of sidewalks, driveways, and paved areas. It creates rust, which is very difficult to remove.

Some common iron supplements are iron sulfate, iron phosphate (which is also a very good snail control material), and blood meal. Blood meal provides iron to your soil while it adds nitrogen. Some signs of iron deficiency include:

- interveinal chlorosis of young foliage— veins remain green while leaves yellow;
- twig and dieback of young growth; and
- tissue death in severe cases.

Zinc

Zinc is taken up by plants as the positively charged zinc cation. It is an important constituent of several enzyme systems, and it controls the synthesis of certain essential plant growth hormones. Zinc is often the micronutrient most often needed in Western soils, and its availability is affected by soil pH, much in the same way iron availability is.

Zinc is supplied to soils and directly to plants. It is available to gardeners and farmers in both liquid and granular forms. Zinc sulfate, which is also a source for sulfur, is one of the most common types of zinc compounds produced for gardening and for farming use. Citrus fruits, grapes, tomatoes, and other tree fruits are known to use large quantities of zinc. Symptoms of zinc deficiency are:

- reduced bud and fruit production;
- crinkling of new growth and a decrease in stem length;
- interveinal chlorosis (often misdiagnosed as an iron deficiency); and
- dieback on year-old growth

Manganese

Manganese is used by plants as the positively charged manganese cation. It is an activator for many enzymes in plant growth processes and assists iron in the formation of chlorophyll during photosynthesis. Yet, high concentrations of manganese may actually suppress iron uptake in plants.

Manganese is commonly applied along with zinc and can be applied to foliage in diluted liquid applications. Citrus and other fruit tree crops are frequently treated with supplemental manganese in the form of manganese sulfate. Manganese supplementation has no commonly recognized requirements and is normally only applied to plants after accurate diagnosis of a deficiency of this mineral. Deficiencies of manganese commonly appear as:

- interveinal discoloring of foliage with veins appearing deeper green—discoloration is not as pronounced as iron chlorosis and is often difficult to detect; and
- gray specks and interveinal white streaks on grasses.

Copper

Copper is the mineral that makes certain types of fruit sweet. It is taken up by plants in two forms of positively charged cations and appears to play a role in the formation of vitamin A in plants. Copper is also an important activator of several plant growth enzymes.

Copper supplementation is rarely needed, and the native supply in many soils is adequate to support plant growth. Highly organic soils and some sandy soils have shown a lack of copper. This mineral is toxic in small amounts, so care should be used when applying copper. Copper sulfate is the most common form of copper supplementation given to soils lacking this mineral.

Copper is also a very beneficial fungicide and is used by many natural gardeners as a dormant spray to prevent diseases from entering plants. It is also used to fight off certain fungal diseases that have already appeared on plants. Cars and trucks entering into many of the avocado groves in California pass through tire dips of copper to prevent the spread of certain rather destructive diseases that attack this valuable fruit crop.

When checking if your soils are deficient in copper, it is a good idea to have a professional soil and plant analysis laboratory determine whether supplementation is required. Symptoms of a copper deficiency in plants include:

- stunted growth;
- death of new growth;
- off-color and poor pigmentation of leaves; and
- wilting and death of leaf tips.

Boron

Boron regulates the metabolism of carbohydrates in plants. Boron is *nonmobile* in plants (much like calcium), meaning that a continual supply is necessary at growing points. Boron is taken up by plants as the negatively charged borate anion. It is known to assist in the differentiation of particular types of stem tissue known as *meristem* tissue.

Boron is often present in toxic amounts in certain arid and semi-arid soils. It is a very good idea to have your soil professionally analyzed before even thinking about adding supplemental boron to your soil. This mineral is commonly found to be deficient in areas of higher rainfall or where summer rains commonly fall. Boron is supplemented to deficient soils in the form of boric acids or other compounds.

Boric acid is also a known way to rid your garden of certain pests such as ants. These uses for boron will be discussed further in our discussion on natural pest control in the garden. Deficiencies of boron appear as:

- thickened, curled, wilted, and chlorotic foliage;
- the death of new and terminal growth, causing what is referred to as a "witches'-broom" effect

- overdevelopment of lateral or side growth after terminal growth has died;
- soft or dead spots on potatoes or other tubers and bulbs; and
- suppressed flowering or improper pollination of flowers.

Molybdenum

Molybdenum is used by plants in the form of the negatively charged molybdate anion. Plants require it so that they may utilize nitrogen. Your plants are unable to transform nitrogen into amino acids without molybdenum being present. Legumes and other nitrogen-fixing plants also cannot fix nitrogen from the atmosphere symbiotically without molybdenum.

Molybdenum is rarely deficient, and is normally only required in ounces per acre when supplementation is necessary. So it is safe to say that this important micronutrient is only required by plants in small amounts to be effective. The most common symptom of a deficiency in molybdenum is stunting of plants and an overall lack of vigor. When plants are deficient in molybdenum, they often look like they need nitrogen. This is due to the key role molybdenum plays in the utilization of nitrogen by your plants.

Chlorine

Chlorine is often more available to plants than is considered healthy. It is required in photosynthetic reactions in plants, and is taken up by them in the form of the negatively charged chloride anion.

Chlorine supplementation is almost never done. This nutrient is universally present in nature and is almost too available (due to the chlorine in the domestic water supply) to suppress bacterial growth. Since this nutrient is so widespread, we won't be suggesting any of the symptoms of deficiency because I don't think it is wise for you to consider supplementation of chlorine under any circumstances. It is good to know that plants use it; otherwise, there would be way too much of this stuff around (even if our clothes were whiter).

As a footnote to this discussion on soil minerals, we should definitely touch on the importance of a balance for plant nutrients in soils. It is critical that a balance of plant nutrients be present in soils, because an abundance of one can create a scenario of reduced uptake of another. Maintaining a balance of nutrients in your soil is an important objective of proper soil management. Judicious use of fertilizers and being mindful of soil pH is critical to ensuring the vigor and health of your garden.

When diagnosing the nutrient needs of your plants, it should be noted that many symptoms of deficiency appear similar in different minerals. If you are unsure of what might be causing your plants to look sickly, consult a professional soil analyst, or contact your local university and see if they can help you. If you feel comfortable making a diagnosis, do it. Remember that one of the most important aspects in determining mineral deficiencies is to know the pH of your soil. This will allow you to make educated assumptions. If you decide that you have made a proper diagnosis of a mineral deficiency in your soil, use small amounts or diluted amounts of that mineral in test areas to see if the health of your plants improves. If it does, it is pretty safe to assume you did it right. Few things are more rewarding than properly diagnosing a problem in your garden. This is one of the many ways natural gardeners get connected with the "nuts and bolts" of how nature works.

Organic Matter

Organic matter is defined as "any material derived from a living or dead plant or animal." The operative element in organic matter is carbon. Carbon has to be present for something to be considered organic, and it is the basis of the discipline of organic chemistry. We will not be focusing too much on the hard science of organic matter, but will instead be considering its role in the soil and how it assists in creating vigor in plant material.

No discussion of the role of organic matter is complete without first touching on the vocabulary used to describe it. Organic matter is often described as *compost, mulch, shavings, humus,* and *manure.*

These descriptions are often interchangeable, and are generalized in favor of brevity. I will be calling each of these items by their name so you can define the differences. When I use the term *fully composted,* I mean exactly that. This term refers to any organic matter that has fully decayed into a stable material. *Fully composted manure* is a term I will use to describe various types of animal poop (feces) that have decayed to the point where they no longer generate much heat from decomposition. These materials have stabilized to a point where they can be applied directly around plants without fear of "burning" plant tissues. I will call some partially decayed materials with larger particle size *mulches.* We will use the term *mulch* to describe these organic materials that are used to cover soils in order to insulate them from the elements. The term *shavings* is used to describe wood products such as sawmill and lumber production waste. We will be using the word *humus* to describe the spongy and stable final stage of decomposition of organic matter. The term *manure* will be use to describe anything that emanates from the backside of an animal. When we describe the manure that is left by birds, we will be using the term *guano.* See how easy it is to get the full scoop on poop?

Soils utilize organic matter in several ways. One of the most basic ways that organic matter serves to increase soil quality is by increasing biological activity. Soils that have optimum levels of organic matter in them also have a high level of biological organisms working and living in them. It is important to note (for those of you attempting to live in a bacteria-free world), that in a healthy soil that is rich in organic matter, more than five billion microbes can inhabit a couple of tablespoons of soil. Also, the vast majority of these organisms are beneficial to you and to the overall health of you garden. So the modern "microbe=bad thing" axiom used by so many of those antibacterial soap makers is wrong. A soil with a healthy population of microbes is considered a "living soil," and natural gardeners do everything they can to achieve it. A soil without life in it is essentially sterile and won't support a natural garden—or any garden for that matter. The microbial life in healthy soils also helps to fight off organisms that can cause diseases or otherwise negatively affect the vigor of your precious plants. So, isn't it a rather sensible thing to add organic matter to your soil whenever possible?

Organic matter also aids in increasing the "friability" of soil. Friable soils are loose, easy to till or dig, and air or water is able to penetrate them without any trouble. Friable soils drain well but also hold enough moisture to support plant growth.

I have a friend, Doug Gore, who bought a new home here in Southern California. When he described the soil to me, he used the term *concrete*, and he said he needed a jackhammer to dig a hole for bedding plants (about four inches deep). I suggested to him that he add a layer of organic matter to his soil about 12 inches thick (along with some minerals) after we had determined which ones were out of balance. He did this, and in less than a year's time he had the most incredible natural garden.

His neighbors were stuck with the same soil they started with and were constantly spending large sums of money on fertilizers that would wash down the street two minutes after their sprinklers came on, so they started asking him how he did it. Doug told them that he just let nature take its course. He started giving advice to his entire street and has become something of a hero to those who listened. He also spent about a tenth of the hard-earned money that his neighbors did, with ten times the results. Doug became a natural gardener out of necessity, because conventional gardening just cost too much money and had a negative impact on the local environment. He started with "concrete" and ended up with a friable soil that he could dig in without any trouble—all because of organic matter and the biological organisms it supported.

Organic matter is also very fertile stuff. Not only does it improve soil structure and quality, it also feeds your plants. The nutrients that remain in decomposed plant and animal material are converted into food by the microbes in the soil for living plants. These subtle nutrients are provided to living plants in the exact way that nature intended. Doesn't that have a nice ring to it! We will be further discussing the topic of how organic matter feeds your plants in Chapter 3.

Humus

Humus is defined as "the well-decomposed, stable part of organic matter in mineral soils." This really does describe humus inadequately. Humus is an incredible building block of life and health in soils. It is a complex, dark brown, amorphous material formed from the residues of organic matter and resynthesized microbial tissue that is resistant to further decomposition. Humus is an important component of soil, and it plays a major role in determining its physical and chemical properties.

Humus is what happens when you continually add organic matter to your soil. It is spongy and holds water very well within its structure. Water storage and dissolved nutrient storage are just two of the ways that humus works for the natural gardener. It stabilizes and assists in the formation of aggregate particles in tight soils, allowing for better air and water penetration. Humus also creates water-holding particles that help to make sandy soils support plants with less need for watering. Humus is another one of those miracles of nature that allows natural gardeners to build great gardens.

Chapter Two

GUANO HAPPENS!

Natural Fertilizers vs. Synthetic Chemical Plant Foods

One of the selling points used by manufacturers of chemical plant foods is that they are more powerful than plant foods derived from natural materials. This couldn't be further from the truth. While it is true that synthetic chemical plant foods can have very high analyses, they are ephemeral, and their nutrients are often lost in runoff water or volatized into the atmosphere soon after they are applied to a garden. Chemical plant foods are commonly antagonistic to balanced mineral content in soils, they kill many of the beneficial microbes that live in soil, and they have this funny tendency to end up in the storm drain system. Synthetic chemicals also do very little if anything to improve the physical quality of soils they are applied to. It has actually been observed that these chemicals actually deplete soils of their mineral and organic wealth. This is exactly the opposite effect of using natural fertilizers.

The man credited with the invention of synthetic plant foods, Justus Von Leibig, at the time of his death, recanted his lifelong pursuit of shortcuts to nature. This is an excerpt of his final testimony, courtesy of Dr. Bargyla Rateaver of San Diego, California:

"I had sinned against the wisdom of our creator, and received just punishment for it. I wanted to improve his handiwork, and in my blindness, I believed that in this wonderful chain of laws, which ties life to the surface of the earth and always keeps it rejuvenated; there might be a link missing that had to be replaced by me—this weak, powerless nothing.

"The law, to which my research on the topsoil led me, states, 'On the outer crust of the earth, under the influence of the sun, organic life shall develop.' And so, the great master and builder gave the fragments of the earth the ability to attract and hold all these elements necessary to feed plants and further serve animals, like a magnet attracts and holds iron particles, so as no piece be lost. Our master enclosed a second law unto this one, through which the plant bearing earth becomes an enormous cleansing apparatus for the water. Through this particular ability, the earth removes from the water all substances harmful to humans and animals—all products of decay and putrefaction, of perished plant and animal generations.

"What might justify my actions is the circumstance, that a man is the product of his time, and he is only able to escape the commonly accepted views if a violent pressure urges him to muster all his strength to struggle free of these chains of error. The opinion that plants draw their food from a solution that is formed in the soil through rainwater, was everyone's belief. It was engraved into my mind. This opinion was wrong and the source of my foolish behavior.

"When a chemist makes a mistake in rating agricultural fertilizers, don't be too critical of his errors, because he has had to base his conclusions upon facts which he can't know from his own experience, but rather, has to take from agricultural texts as true and reliable. After I learned the reason why my fertilizers weren't effective in the proper way, I was like a person that received a new life. For along with that, all processes of tillage were now explained as to their natural laws. Now that this principle is known and clear to all eyes, the only thing that remains is the astonishment of why it hadn't been

discovered a long time ago. The human spirit, however, is a strange thing. Whatever doesn't fit into the given circle of thinking, doesn't exist."

I know this was a little long, but it's important to see that the "father" of modern chemical fertilizers actually referred to them as folly when confessing his alleged sins. He created a school of thought that we now refer to as *conventional agriculture.* Isn't it unfortunate that this poor, repentant soul didn't have time left at the end of his life to discredit himself publicly? If he had, natural gardening would be called *conventional,* and the chemicals would be considered *fringe.* People grew amazing gardens before the advent of synthetic chemicals; natural gardeners are just continuing with that wisdom and adding a little modern know-how to the process.

Natural fertilizers not only support healthy plant growth, but they build better-quality soil, feed beneficial soil organisms, release their food to plants slowly, and they don't run off into the local lakes or ocean. No chemical plant food can boast so many attributes. Yes, it is true that an analysis of certain chemical plant foods has shown that they have a few more nutrients, but natural plant foods have a subtle activity that chemistry will never provide.

N-P-K

When you look at almost any bag, box, or can of plant food, there are three numbers on the container. Those three numbers express the amounts of the three recognized major plant nutrients. Those three nutrients are: nitrogen-N, phosphorus-P, and potassium-K. The letters N- P-K are the symbols for these nutrients on the periodic table of the elements. The numbers on the package express the percentages of these nutrients. If a fertilizer container has the numbers 15-15-15 on it, this means the material in the container is 15% nitrogen, 15% phosphorus, and 15% potassium. A material that has a zero on the bag in any of those three locations has no measured amount of that particular nutrient. Natural fertilizers and chemical plant foods are all measured this way. Materials that have various amounts of each of these three elements are known as *complete plant foods.*

The term *complete plant food* was invented by the chemical man-ufacturers and could not be more deceptive. We learned in the last chapter that many other nutrients are needed to make a complete plant food. This is another place where natural fertilizers can prevail. They have a wider variety of the minerals in them that are derived from the life they came from. This labeling of N-P-K plant foods as complete plant foods is like your doctor telling you that Twinkies are a complete food. N-P-K merely lists the amounts of three essential nutrients that plants use a lot of in order to grow. If you approach plant foods with this in mind, these numbers can be very helpful in choosing appropriate fertilizers for your garden.

Chemical Fertilizers, Pollution, and Soil Microflora

When a gardener uses chemically produced plant foods to feed his or her garden, there are some risks. These materials often have a very high N-P-K analysis and can be very dangerous to plants when used improperly. Chemical burns from using too much of these mate-rials is a very common occurrence and is often the cause of plant death in the home garden. Overuse of these materials isn't limited to plant damage and death.

When chemical plant foods are used on soils that do not perco-late well—such as clays and silts—they have a tendency to run off after dissolving in rainwater or from irrigation. These dissolved nutri-ents enter into the floodwater control or storm drain system and end up in local watersheds or at the beach. These nutrients then cause unnatural blooms of certain bacteria that can be harmful to human health. Certain rather annoying types of algae are also known to grow somewhat rampant when these nutrients run amok. These algae blooms have the added effect of clouding our lakes a lovely green color so that extra chemicals need to be added to the water before it can come out of our tap clear. At the shore of the ocean is where these algae and bacteria do their most insidious work. The entire tidal zone from estuaries to the surf is affected by the entry of these nutri-ents into their midst. Water clarity is affected, harmful bacteria and disease organisms multiply at an unnatural rate, and the water becomes unhealthy to swim in. Then we get to see those familiar and unfortunate signs on our beaches and bays that warn us that our oceans are too contaminated for us to enjoy. This environmental impact is nothing compared to what these added nutrients do to the sea life and to life in the tidal zone.

When I was a child growing up on the beach in San Diego County, we used to spend all of our time at the seashore. The life in the ocean was amazing. At low tide, we would check out the life in the tidepools. There was so much life in those confined spaces that we could spend hours just checking out a particular pool that was no bigger than a Jacuzzi and only a few inches deep. There were clams, sand crabs, and sand dollars all over the place. Fishermen used to catch all kinds of cool stuff that swam in the surf.

Today at those same beaches, all that low tide reveals is an abundance of bright green filamentitious algae that chokes out all other life. It looks like a lawn was planted where a wonderful diversity of life once thrived. This observation has prompted concerned individuals to form groups such as the Surfrider Foundation, Trout Unlimited, Greenpeace, and The Audubon Society. Hopefully we can see those tidepools full of life again thanks to the efforts of organizations such as these.

The above are just a few of the environmental problems caused by the use and misuse of chemical and synthetic plant foods. Another story of biological suppression occurs in the soil itself.

Chemical plant foods suppress the growth of diverse biological organisms in soil in favor of the few organisms capable of using these high-powered materials. Many of the microbes in the soil whose growth is stimulated by chemical plant foods crowd out and suffocate other microflora. Then when the nutrients are gone, which isn't a very long time, these microbes die off and make way for fermenting bacteria that have pathogenic behaviors, often to the detriment of the plants in your garden. A healthy, living soil depends on a wide diversity of microscopic organisms. Chemical plant foods are antagonistic to this biological diversity. Justus Von Leibig finally realized that the soil is an incredibly effective filter for pollutants. But when you tax the filter beyond its capacity, where do the pollutants go?

Natural gardeners strive to sustain this balance of biology in soil so the filter remains healthy and functioning properly. Just the way nature intended!

Types of Natural Plant Foods

I am frequently told by avid users of chemical plant foods that they would gladly use natural fertilizers if there were any that performed the specific functions specialized chemicals do. I reply by showing them a list of dozens of materials that are capable of sustaining plant growth while they correct any number of soil mineral imbalances, neutralize soil pH, and improve soil quality. That list of natural plant foods is included below. I have described each of these materials with some handy information about them, and which nutrients they supply to plants.

Alfalfa Meal

Alfalfa meal is derived from cut and dried alfalfa and then ground into a granular meal. Alfalfa is one of those nitrogen-fixing legumes we talked about earlier. It has an average N-P-K rating of 4-1-1 and is known to supply an abundance of trace minerals, as well as the big three. Alfalfa also provides a growth-stimulating hormone called *triconatol*. This is one of your rose garden's favorite natural fertilizers and is a great addition to the compost heap to supplement nitrogen and speed decomposition of organic matter. Alfalfa meal can feed your plants for up to four months and is considered an extremely valuable ingredient in blended natural fertilizer mixes. Application rates for alfalfa meal range between 2 and 5 pounds per 100 square feet of garden space (approximately 10' x 10'). Vegetarian gardeners who are conscious of using animal products in the garden can use alfalfa meal as a primary plant food.

Azomite

This material has become increasingly popular among natural gardeners and is referred to as a "rock dust." Rock dusts such as azomite have been in use for many years and are known for their ability to supply a wealth of trace minerals (micronutrients) to soils and plants. Azomite also has the added benefit of raising pH in acidic soils. Apply azomite at a rate of $1/2$ to 2 pounds per 10 square feet of garden space. This material is especially effective on citrus and other fruit trees. Azomite is also used in animal feeds to increase health in livestock. If you have laying chickens running in the yard to control pests, feed them a little azomite. It will increase eggshell strength and impart a greater mineral content to the edible parts.

Bat Guano

This fast-acting natural plant food is a very good source for nitrogen. Bat guano is one of the most powerful of all the natural animal manures, and although bats are not birds; their poop is called *guano*. It has an N-P-K rating that averages 10-2-1, but can vary depending on the geography of the cave where it is collected and the primary diet of the bats. This material is one of my favorite lawn foods and can last as long as two months. Application rates for bat guano vary from 3 to 5 pounds of material per 100 square feet of garden space. I love making a tea out of this material for plants. I take about three tablespoons of bat guano and put it into a piece of cheesecloth or a square of nylon stocking to make a tea bag. I then drop it into a gallon of water and let it sit in the sun for several hours. The tea that is made from this is a great plant reviver and really works well when watering newly transplanted plants to get them going. Bat guano also has about 20 trace minerals in it to benefit your plants and soil.

Blood Meal

This by-product of the meat-packing industry is kiln dried and packaged as a valuable source of nitrogen, iron, and a number of other essential trace minerals (micronutrients) present in blood. This material has been used for years and years by natural gardeners to boost plant growth. Blood meal has an average N-P-K analysis of 13-0-0 and is mostly used to boost nitrogen to promote plant growth. It is a valuable addition to the compost heap to speed up decomposition. Blood meal is used at a rate of 5 to 10 pounds per 100 square feet of garden space. When using this product in an area where dogs run, be careful. Dogs love this stuff and will dig in the garden in areas where it is applied, even if your puppies are not diggers. This stuff brings out the wolf in any dog. I love to use blood meal in blended natural fertilizers to increase the nitrogen levels when needed.

Bone Meal

This material is a very popular natural source of phosphorus and calcium. Bone meal also contains a number of valuable trace minerals essential for healthy plant growth. There is a trick with bone meal. The finer it is ground, the faster it lends its nutrients to the soil and to your plants. People who have planted bulbs and have used bone meal know how well it promotes flowering of plants. A typical N-P-K analysis for bone meal is 1-11-0 with up to 22% available calcium. Standard application rates for bone meal are 3 to 10 pounds per 100 square feet of garden space.

A little primer on Mad Cow Disease: Since bovine spongiform encephelopathy (Mad Cow Disease) was discovered in Europe a few years ago, there has been a lot of talk in the gardening community about contaminated bone meal. It is true that bone meal does come from ground-up bones, and it is also true that cattle bones make up a significant portion of the raw materials used in making bone meal. I have heard arguments from both sides of the fence and have yet to hear of any bone meal being imported from Europe, or any cases of Mad Cow Disease being transmitted through an asparagus. This is one of those areas where gardeners will have to make up their own minds as to the use of this material.

Boron Supplements

When we discussed boron in the previous chapter, I said that this essential mineral rarely needs to be supplemented and should only be applied if a professional analysis of soils or plant tissues indicates a deficiency. It is often only applied at very small rates (2 to 10 pounds per acre on farmlands), so you can see how little would be used in a garden. This is why I recommend that home gardeners only use a water-soluble boron supplement. In this way, it can be applied in very controlled amounts. For this reason, I like a material called *Solubor,* which can be found at most farm supply stores. When soil analysis says that boron levels are low but not bad, use kelp products or certain rock dusts that have minute amounts of boron in them. Then, you don't have to buy a 50-pound bag of a material you will only use a few ounces of.

Brix Supplements

Brix is another new word we are going to be using often in this book. It is pronounced "Bricks," and is the term used to identify the amount of natural plant sugars that occur within the tissue of plants. This is an important part of natural gardening because brix levels are often an indicator of overall plant health and a primary method of determining disease and pest resistance. A brix level is the result of a balanced diet. Kelp products; and rock dusts such as azomite, calcium supplements, and fossilized kelp (a rock dust and a kelp product), are very handy for ensuring that brix levels are high in your plants. Brix is also an indicator of how sweet your fruits and vegetables will be. High brix means high plant sugars, which means a sweet harvest. We will be discussing the importance of brix levels further when we cover natural pest- and disease-control techniques. This is another one of those secret terms that avid gardeners use. But it isn't a secret to *you!*

Canola Meal

This valuable source of nitrogen is less well known than some of the other vegetable sources of plant food. Canola seed hulls are a by-product of the manufacturing of canola oil. The average N-P-K analysis of this material is 6-2-1, and it is very rich in proteins that are valuable to plants.

Apply canola meal to gardens at a rate of 3 to 5 pounds per 100 square feet. This material can last up to four months and is also an excellent soil quality-enhancing material. I sometimes use it in blended mixes when I can find it.

Chelated Minerals

Chelates are very stable organic materials that may contain a high concentration of several minerals, or a single mineral. They are often associated with metallic minerals such as iron, zinc, copper, manganese, and molybdenum. These are very powerful materials and should only be used if a deficiency of one of these minerals is negatively affecting plant health. These materials can be in solid or liquid form and are often used in fertilizer injection systems in commercial agriculture. The home gardener can benefit from combination chelated mineral products sold at most garden centers or by the single mineral chelates if soil conditions dictate their use. A professional soil analysis should precede the use of these materials. Chelated minerals are rapidly available to plants and should be used in small amounts suggested by the label on the package or by the laboratory that performed the soil analysis. These are very valuable nutrient sources for plants.

Chicken Manure (Guano)

This is one of the most widely recognized natural plant fertilizers and has been used by gardeners and farmers for centuries to grow healthy plants. Chicken manure is a good source of nitrogen, phosphorus, potassium, and many trace minerals. The average N-P-K of composted chicken manure is 2-4-2. This material is very close to being a complete plant food and is very effective in sustaining ample nutrition for plants in soil. Chicken manure contains the essential amino acids, proteins, and enzymes that plants require. This material also helps to keep the beneficial microbes in your soil happy as well. Use chicken manure at a rate of 10 to 20 pounds per 100 square feet of garden. Remember to use fully composted material; fresh chicken manure can be really strong and cause plants to burn. Fresh material is also very often high in soluble sodium and chlorine. This can be a problem, so use composted material. You'll be happier, and your garden will, too.

Chilean Nitrate of Soda

This is a very powerful material that is mined from natural deposits in South America. This material contains 16% nitrogen in a very fast-acting form. The only drawback is that it also contains over 26% sodium, which can be very toxic to plants in such concentrations—especially in soils such as silts and clays, which do not percolate well. Gardeners need to be very careful with this material, yet it is very useful in the right conditions. Application rates for nitrate of soda are between $1/2$ to 1 pound per 100 square feet of garden space.

Commercial Composts

These are the composts that you buy in bags at the nursery or in bulk quantities from manufacturers. Commercial composts are generally very good organic materials and have an average N-P-K of 1-1-1.

Composts also provide virtually every known mineral used by plants. The fertility of these products is often overlooked in favor of their value as soil conditioners, or simply as a source of organic matter to improve soil quality. However, composts are very fertile materials, and although they are definitely an excellent source of organic matter, don't look past their abilities to impart nutrition to plants.

Composts come in a wide variety of types and are often derived from recycled organic materials picked up at your doorstep. The facilities that many of our communities provide to take in yard waste (commonly called *greenwaste*) frequently sell their composted material to companies that package it and sell it back to us.

Other materials, incorrectly called composts, are derived from wood products and should be called *shavings*. These products are sometimes injected with ammonia gas to accelerate decomposition, so they don't use nitrogen in the soil in order to break down. I don't use these materials, and they are not recognized as natural or organic due to the use of chemical ammonia in their manufacturing process. If you have access to wood shavings, try to find out if ammonia has been used on them. If not, add some manure or guano to them, and then use them in the garden. Natural organic matter is a good thing; the use of chemicals to fool the consumer is not.

Corn Gluten Meal

This amazing material is a very efficient source of nitrogen from a vegetable source, so vegetarian gardeners may feel more comfortable using it. It has an N-P-K analysis of 10-0-0, and the nitrogen it provides is rather fast-acting. Typical application rates for this material are 2 to 4 pounds per 100 square feet of garden, and 3 to 5 pounds per 100 square feet of lawn area.

This material has an added benefit to natural gardeners. Corn gluten contains powerful *allelopathic* (meaning "growth retarding") properties that can actually work on behalf of us gardeners to control the germination of weed seeds. One thing to know, the allelopathic substances in this material do not differentiate between weed seeds and seeds you want to grow. Corn gluten meal will, however, effectively control the germination of weeds in established plantings and can do wonders for unwanted weeds such as dandelions in your lawn. This material is one of the many secrets we natural gardeners have and one of the ways in which we control weeds without resorting to a hoe. Corn gluten meal is normally available at feed stores and can be found at organic gardening and farming supply companies (see the Resources section). The weed-retarding properties in corn gluten meal last between one and four months and are capable of lasting longer in cooler temperatures and in heavy soils. Who needs chemical pre-emergent herbicides when nature provides perfectly effective materials that don't pollute?

Cottonseed Meal

Cottonseed meal is considered to be one of the most versatile natural plant foods extracted from plant residues. This is also one of the most widely sold of all of the natural fertilizers and can be found at almost any garden center. Cottonseed meal has an average N-P-K analysis of 6-2-1.5 and is very good at gradually lowering soil pH. Gardeners that love to grow acid-loving plants such as azaleas, camellias, and those finicky gardenias will find that this is a perfect plant food for their needs. It is also fairly long-lasting and continues to release its nutrients for four to six months. Those gardeners who would like to try their hand at growing blueberries should consider using cottonseed meal as a primary food source because blueberries like it acid. Gardeners with alkaline soils also like cottonseed meal because it slowly neutralizes alkaline pH conditions.

Cottonseed meal is an excellent addition to many blended natural fertilizer mixes. Its long-lasting nature allows natural gardeners to spend more time enjoying the garden and less time feeding it. Application rates for cottonseed meal average between 5 to 10 pounds per 100 square feet of garden space and can be applied at rates of up to 20 pounds per 100 square feet.

Dolomite Lime

Gardeners with low soil pH that is also deficient in magnesium often use dolomite lime. It should not be used in soils that are alkaline, and one should never assume they have a magnesium deficiency. This is a good time to remember Professor Allbrecht's work on calcium and magnesium in soils. Too much magnesium can cause a lot of problems and wreak havoc on the structure and friability of soils. It is always a good idea to get a professional analysis of your soil before adding magnesium supplements.

Dolomite lime is a very good source of both calcium and magnesium that averages 45% calcium and 35% magnesium in carbonate form, which is readily available for assimilation into the soil solution. Apply this material to soils at rates from 1 to 10 pounds per 100 square feet of garden. This material sometimes requires yearly application or should be applied before working to soil so it is fully incorporated.

Feather Meal

Feather meal is a very useful source of slow-releasing and long-lasting nitrogen for plants. It is made from ground-up feathers and is very high in available proteins. Feather meal has an N-P- K of 12-0-0 and can last as long as nine months. It has no odor to speak of and is a very good material for feeding lawns.

Apply feather meal to the garden at a rate of 2 to 5 pounds per 100 square feet. Feed your lawn with this material at a rate of 5 to 7 pounds per 100 square feet. I often use feather meal in blended fertilizer mixes to add a longer-lasting source of nitrogen so that feeding only needs to be done once a season.

Fish Emulsion

It may smell funny and have an odor that lingers for a few hours, but fish emulsion is one of the most fertile substances available to the natural gardener. It is widely regarded as a good plant food by conventional chemical users as well. Fish emulsion is a very good natural plant food for gardeners who garden outdoors with containers. It is easy to use and supplies a number of trace minerals to plants, including chlorine. It has an average N-P-K analysis of 5-2-2 and lasts for up to two months. Fish emulsion is often sold as "fish solubles" and can be found at every garden center, anywhere.

I have yet to find a plant that doesn't respond well to feeding with this material. It can be applied when you water your container plants, and it helps to keep potting soils fresh and loose. I use fish emulsion at varying rate from 2 to 10 tablespoons per gallon of water depending on the crop or plant I'm feeding.

Fish Meal

This is one of my favorite plant foods. Fish meal has an N-P-K analysis of 10-4-0 and lasts for up to eight months. It should be applied to gardens at a rate of up to 5 pounds per 100 square feet. I use fish meal often when transplanting new plants. I put some in the backfill mix and forget about the plant for six months or so and am never disappointed with the results. Fish meal is also a very good material to feed your plants when they look a bit sickly. It really gives slow-growing plants a boost!

Fish meal is a very good addition to many blended natural fertilizer mixes as a source of fast-acting and long-lasting nitrogen, along with a number of other trace minerals. It has a pungent odor of fish and should be used at a distance from windows. The odor only lasts for a day or so, and it is worth the temporary inconvenience for the health of your garden.

Granite Dust

This material is one of the rock dusts that is currently catching the natural gardening community on fire. Since mineral content in soils has become recognized as a major contributor to sustained plant and soil health, natural gardeners have started using these materials to supplement those minerals. Granite dust has an N-P-K analysis averaging 0-0-4 and contains an abundance of trace minerals. This material can last up to seven years in your soil. Apply granite dust at a rate of up to 10 pounds per 100 square feet of garden space.

Greensand

Greensand is a mineral material that is mined in a few places around the world. The most famous deposit of this mineral that geologists call "glauconite" is in New Jersey. New Jersey greensand is extracted from a 70- to 80-million-year-old marine deposit, which consists of iron-potassium-silicates and an incredible abundance of trace minerals. Greensand is a very long-lasting material with a very slow release. Do not use greensand if you need potassium and iron fast. This material can take as long as a year to begin working but will last for ten years. Patience counts.

I apply greensand at rates of up to 10 pounds per 100 square feet of garden. I only use very small amounts of this material, so I can use it year after year without getting too much accumulation of minerals. I frequently add small amounts of greensand to my blended natural plant foods, and in the recipe chapter, you will get a chance to do it as well.

I know a farmer who used greensand to supplement iron for his citrus groves. Three years after he had applied the material to his crop, his trees were the envy of all of the neighboring groves, and his organic fruit commanded the highest prices he had ever gotten because of the high quality of his crop. The growers that used chemicals in his area asked him what he had done. He responded by telling them about greensand and was laughed at. He told me that his groves continued to produce super-quality fruit on healthy trees for five more years until a hard frost ruined his crop. He reapplied greensand later that year, and the success of his groves continues today. He told me he learned about it from reading an organic gardening magazine. Farmers do learn things from us, and we should learn something from this farmer.

Gypsum

Gypsum is a common calcium material frequently used to supplement sulfur to soils as well. It is a mined material that is also used in the making of drywall. Gypsum is a material known also as calcium sulfate and is used in areas where pH is normally high to supplement calcium. It is also used to open up compacted clay and silt soils in the gardens of Southern California's urban sprawl gardens. This material averages 20% calcium and 17% sulfur. One of the great parts about using gypsum in soils that have an abundance of magnesium is that the sulfur in it ties up excess magnesium, allowing for better mineral exchanges in the soil. Apply gypsum to the garden at rates up to 15 pounds per 100 square feet.

Hoof and Horn Meal

Most gardeners whom I know would rather enjoy their gardens than work in them. Hoof and horn meal allows natural gardeners to do just that. This by-product of the beef industry is actually ground hooves and horns. It is an extremely rich and long-lasting source of nitrogen for the natural garden. Most hoof and horn meal has an N-P-K analysis of 13.5-0-0 and will continue to feed plants for up to 12 months. Like feather meal, hoof and horn meal is very rich in proteins and also supplies some calcium to plants. The warning I gave about dogs when we discussed blood meal also goes for this material. The scent of this stuff, and boy, does it have a scent, drives dogs bonkers. They roll in it, eat it, and frolic in it like they're in dog heaven.. The odor lasts for a few days, and one should be prepared for it. The payoff is that it lasts so long and works so well.

Apply hoof and horn meal to the garden in the late fall or very early spring. It takes about six weeks to start working, and if applied in the late fall, it will have all winter in the soil to transmit its abundance into the soil. When spring has sprung and plants are actively using nitrogen, hoof and horn meal will have provided ample supplies. There is no need to reapply until the following year. Hoof and horn meal can be applied to gardens at rates up to 5 pounds per 100 square feet. This is one of my favorite materials to add to blended natural fertilizers in order to extend their activity.

Humates and Humic Acids

These materials are actually the fossil remains of prehistoric plants and animals. Humates are carbon-rich materials that provide an excellent source of humus to soils where they are applied. Humates and humic acids improve the structure of soils low in organic matter and increase the nutrient- and moisture-holding capacity of sandy soils. Apply these valuable materials to soils at rates between 10 and 15 pounds per 100 square feet of garden space. Humates can average more than 35% stable organic matter. Humic acids can also be found in liquid forms and can be applied directly to soils through fertilizer injection equipment. Farmer and natural gardeners have been using these products for years to boost the organic matter content of their soils.

Iron Sulfate

This powerful source of iron and sulfur is often used in soils that have a high pH to reduce alkalinity, while supplying a very strong amount of these two minerals. Iron sulfate contains a minimum of 20% iron and 20% sulfur. Normal application rates for this material range from $1/2$ to 2 pounds per 100 square feet of garden space. Be careful using this material around sidewalks and any area where you don't want rust to show up. This product makes rust appear in the most unfortunate places when it touches them.

Kelp, Fossilized, Liquid Extracts, and Kelp Meal

Every natural gardener should be using kelp materials in conjunction with their regular fertilization programs. Decades of research and field trials have confirmed the role of kelp in increasing crop yields, drought resistance, frost protection, and stress recovery in plants. Although these materials do have some nitrogen, phosphorus, and potassium, their value is not as a fertilizer but as a growth stimulant. Kelp products contain potent concentrations of trace minerals, amino acids, and many growth hormones that stimulate cell division and the development of healthy plants and root systems. Liquid extracts can be applied directly to the foliage of plants. Kelp meals and rock dusts from fossil kelp deposits are applied to soils. All of these materials are valuable and should be considered to be an integral part of your natural gardening bag of tricks.

Liquid kelp extracts are very versatile materials that can be applied directly to plant foliage and are very good at providing quick results when plants are stressed or otherwise weakened by heat, cold, or an apparent lack of nutrients. In its liquid form, kelp will supply your plants with an abundant supply of plant growth-stimulating enzymes, amino acids, and hormones. I often tell people who have sickly houseplants to apply liquid kelp to the foliage of these sad creatures. The revival rate is astonishing. I love to add a little of this material to manure and guano teas, as well as fish emulsion to ensure that plants are getting a truly balanced and complete nutritional supplement. I use this material according to the instructions on the bottle, as strength varies with manufacturer. When I add it to manure teas, I use it at one-third to one-half strength.

Kelp meal is a longer-lasting supply of all of the nutrients that liquid kelp provides. It takes more time to work as well. Kelp meal is a good supply of potassium with an average N-P-K analysis of 0-0-3, along with the same abundance of trace minerals and growth stimulators. I normally apply kelp meal to soils in the fall or winter to allow ample time before spring for it to release its abundant value. I do this so that when warm weather sets in and plants begin actively growing, there is a steady supply of these nutrients available to them. As with liquid kelp and fossilized kelp, kelp meal also supplies the microbes and larger beneficial organisms in the soil with essential vitamins and minerals. I like to add kelp meal to blended natural fertilizer mixes to boost trace mineral content and to supply the bounty of growth-stimulating hormones that plants so gratefully accept and eagerly use. Typical application rates for kelp meal are between 1 to 2 pounds per 100 square feet of garden space. This material can last up to 12 months. Remember that this is a powerful material, and a little goes a long way.

Fossilized kelp is mined from ancient seabeds and contains all of the mineral wealth that other kelp materials have, with the added bonus of a rich supply of calcium. I found out about this material from old Native American and pioneer tales. It had been used by prairie farmers for centuries and was actually transported from neighboring tribe to neighboring tribe as a commodity and crop productivity aid. It was in use by some natural farmers but had little notoriety. It was marketed as Kelzyme, fossilized kelp.

Since the mid-'80s, Kelzyme has been used by farmers to supplement their soils with an abundant supply of trace minerals, plant growth stimulators, and calcium. It is now used on rice, wine and table grapes, fruit orchards, vegetables, wheat, and as a soil conditioner. Kelzyme is also used as a feed supplement for livestock, and is also packaged in capsule form for human use. I have used it as a lime alternative and as a gypsum alternative when supplementing calcium in soils. This material actually has a higher calcium analysis than either lime or gypsum (over 40% calcium), and is assimilated into soil very quickly. It lasts a long time and frequently only requires reapplication every other year or every third year. I do like to apply this material every season, normally in the fall, to soils where there is a lot of plant activity, like the veggie garden. I apply this material to soils at an average rate of 1 to 5 pounds per 100 square feet of garden space. I also add this material to blended fertilizer mixes in order to ensure an ample supply of essential plant nutrients.

Studies on the benefits of using kelp materials have been carried out to determine their capabilities in disease- and pest-resistance enhancement. It is apparent from the results of these tests that kelp products and especially the fossil kelp materials appear to reduce susceptibility to certain common plant diseases by promoting the health of beneficial organisms in the soil while strengthening cell wall strength. Some researchers are now focusing on the role of the iodine that is in these products in the suppression of certain disease organisms, while promoting greater metabolic health in plants where kelp is used.

Lime

Lime is an old standby for correcting the pH of acidic soils. It can be derived from the shells of marine creatures (oysters) or from mined deposits of limestone. Calcium is the primary mineral supplied by this material. Lime is used to supplement calcium and is very quickly assimilated into the soil solution. It is a very useful material and is rather inexpensive to use and easy to apply to both large and small areas, since the advent of mechanical drop spreaders. Apply lime to your garden at rates between 2 to 10 pounds per 100 square feet. Certain types of lime may have a tendency to be somewhat high in lead, so inquire as to the content of this potentially harmful element when buying a liming material.

Magnesium Sulfate

Magnesium sulfate, also known as Epsom salts, is a very potent source of essential magnesium without the pH-buffering capabilities of dolomite limestone. This material is more neutral in pH. Epsom salts are highly water-soluble and can be applied when watering plants in need of magnesium. It contains an average magnesium analysis of 10% and about 6% sulfate sulfur. The magnesium in Epsom salts are readily available to plants and should be used with caution so as not to overdose your soil with magnesium, thus creating scenarios where other nutrient availability is suppressed. Application rates vary from 1 to 3 pounds per 100 square feet in granular form, and 1 to 4 tablespoons per gallon of water when applied as a liquid. I use caution with this material because many organic certification agencies do not recognize Epsom salts as a natural product because it is sometimes manufactured chemically.

Micronized Plant Growth Stimulants

These new products are changing the way natural and organic farmers and gardeners apply nutrients to their plants. These products are ground to ultrafine powders that can be suspended in water and run through fertilizer injector/irrigation systems without the fear of clogging the irrigation system. Humates, mineral supplements, rock dusts, and organic compost concentrates are micronized in order for them to be conveniently applied through the irrigation water. These new materials are very useful for you gardeners who grow plants in containers, and for those of you looking for nonchemical ways to feed your houseplants without having to deal with the odor of some natural plant foods. Micronized plant nutrients are gaining in popularity and will soon be available at more places than farm supply stores and specialty growers supply warehouses.

Rock Phosphate

This material is a rich source of phosphorus. Rock phosphate also contains a good source of calcium and iron in many cases. The average N-P-K analysis is 0-25-0, with 30% calcium, 3% iron, and a number of trace minerals. Rock phosphate may raise soil pH somewhat and should be used carefully in alkaline soils to ensure proper pH management. Typical application rates for rock phosphate is between 3 to 6 pounds per 100 square feet of garden space. Rock phosphate comes in two primary forms, soft and hard rock phosphate. Soft rock phosphate is more readily available to plants, but hard rock has a longer-lasting effect. I use soft rock phosphate in many of the blended plant food mixes I make and find it to be a superior material. This material can last as long as five years when applied alone to soils deficient in phosphorus.

Seabird Guano

Yes, this is exactly what it sounds like—pelican poop. For those of you who have been dive-bombed by a militant seagull or seen one of those white-capped islands off of the coast, this is what is used to feed your plants. The most popular sources for this material are from South America—namely, Chile and Peru. Seabird guano can come in a variety of analyses. Some materials are very high in available nitrogen, while others are high in phosphorus. N-P-K analyses can run from 12-8-2 to 1-10-0. I really like these materials, but have some reservations on how they are harvested. The impact on the birds has not been positive, and many of the operations that harvest this material exercise little regard for the environment or for the birds that make this valuable material. Application rates for seabird guano vary from 3 to 10 pounds per 100 square feet of garden space, and an amazing tea can be made from this material using the same recipe for bat guano tea.

Shrimp Shell Meal

This is a by-product of seafood processing and is an excellent source of a wide variety of plant nutrients. An average N-P-K analysis of shrimp meal is 5-8-15, with a rich source of calcium and other trace minerals. Shrimp shell meal also contains chitin, which is what shells are made of. Because of this chitin, shrimp shell meal also increases the populations of chitin-eating microbes that live in the soil. These organisms can reduce populations of pest nematodes and other pests that live in the soil. Typical application rates for shrimp shell meal is between 10 to 15 pounds per 100 square feet of garden space. This material also contains iodine, which is being investigated as a disease suppressant. Shrimp shell meal has an odor, so be prepared. I love to mix this material into some of my favorite natural plant food blends.

Soil Sulfur

This material will lower high soil pH faster than any other soil conditioner. Soil sulfur averages 90% elemental sulfur and can be as high as 99% pure. Application of this material should be done with the supervision or with direction of a professional soil analysis. A little sulfur stimulates soil microbiology; a lot is toxic and can cause a myriad of problems. Apply soil sulfur at rates between 1 to 5 pounds per 100 square feet of garden space depending on soil pH and sulfur content. In alkaline soils, there is no other material more effective for bringing pH back down toward neutral. And remember that neutral pH is when nutrients are most available to plants.

Sul-Po-Mag, K-Mag

Geologists call this extremely valuable mineral "langbeinite." Sul-po-mag is a rich source for sulfur, potassium, and magnesium, with an N-P-K analysis of 0-0-22 and 22% sulfur as well as 11% magnesium. Roses love this stuff! Sul-po-mag is a much longer-lasting source of magnesium than Epsom salts (magnesium sulfate). All organic certification organizations accept this material, so there is no guessing as to its origin. It is a concentrated material, and average application rates are about 1 pound per 100 square feet of garden space. I add this material to many blended natural plant foods because it is so good at supplying potassium to plants as well.

Sulfate of Potash

This highly concentrated source of potassium has an N-P-K analysis of 0-0-50, with 18% sulfur. Sulfate of potash is a rather fast-release material and should not be applied to gardens at rates higher than 1 to 2 pounds per 100 square feet unless otherwise recommended by a professional soil lab.

Wood Ash

This is not charcoal ash from the barbecue. Wood ash is most valuable to plants when young plant tissue is the source of the material. This is a material high in trace minerals and carbon. It will raise soil pH when used, so be careful in alkaline soils. The N-P-K analysis of wood ash is highly variable, averaging 0-4-13 with consistent amounts of available copper, zinc, manganese, iron, sulfur, and boron. Application rates average from 1 to 3 pounds per 100 square feet of garden space. Wood ash last up to 12 months in soils.

<u>Worm Castings</u>

This is one of the best natural soil conditioners known. Worm castings are actually earthworm poops. They are rich in humus and are a valuable source of organic matter in a very stable form. It just seems that the more we learn about earthworms, the more valuable they are to our gardens. Aristotle called them "the plows of the Earth," but I like to think of earthworms as a natural gardener's herd of full-time roto-tillers. Castings are somewhat variable in nutrient content and can contain a lot of soil in them. Be careful that you pick a reputable source for worm castings, and once you find a good one, make sure to use it. Worm castings can be applied at rates of up to 3 cubic feet per 100 square feet of garden space. This is one of the best soil conditioners for sandy soils. A couple of teaspoons added to your potted plants will keep potting soils fresh and better able to hold on to nutrients and water. One of the best things about using worm castings is that hundreds of earthworm cocoons are in them that hatch out to your own earthworm population. This may be the very best thing natural gardeners can do for their soil.

<u>Zinc Sulfate</u>

This material averages 36% zinc and 18% sulfur. It is a very valuable mineral supplement in areas where zinc is low in soils. Most zinc sulfate materials are water-soluble and can be applied directly to foliage after proper dilution. Use of this concentrated material should be supervised or directed by a soil analyst.

This litany of natural materials is one of the reasons why when some "expert" tells me that there are not enough good natural products available to adequately support and sustain healthy plant growth, I have to be amused. The materials mentioned in this section are all of great value to natural gardeners of all skill levels and should give you an idea of how many different materials are available to improve the health of your garden.

We will discuss some blended natural plant food mixes in each of the following chapters on caring for particular types of gardens.

How Natural Fertilizers Feed the Soil and
Let the Soil Feed Your Plants

Natural plant foods work by promoting the vigor of an entire biological ecosystem in microscopic scale. The nutrients provided in natural fertilizers feed organisms that feed other microbes, which excrete enzymes and amino acids that feed further organisms up the chain, eventually feeding your plants. This process has been perfected over the last four billion years; I have a hard time arguing with that kind of success.

A natural garden uses this perfection and feeds each individual member of this ecosystem in order to sustain the vigor of the entire system. The complexities of this process are far too numerous to detail in the time we have together in the garden. However, we do have time to say that it is pretty safe that if you concentrate on using mild and subtle strategies for plant and soil health that you will ensure healthy soil ecology in your gardens. The myriad of biological activity in soil has specific effects on your plants! Health! Just the way nature intended.

Chapter Three

COMPOST AND MULCH, A NATURAL GARDENER'S BEST FRIENDS

What Is the Difference Between Compost and Mulch?

The answer to this question is fairly simple. The difference between compost and mulch is determined by the amount of decomposition of the organic matter in either of these two materials. Compost is simply fully decomposed organic matter that is prepared to be integrated into soil in order to form humus. Mulch, on the other hand, is normally less decomposed and is placed on top of soil to conserve moisture and protect soil from the elements while suppressing weeds. Now for the silly part.

Composts can be used as mulches, and mulches can become compost as they decompose in place on top of the soil. Confusing enough? Let's try for more. Mulches are often put on top of soils in a practice called *sheet composting,* where layers of mulch are placed on top of soil. Let's face it—compost and mulch are both materials that supply needed organic matter to soils. The difference is purely in how far rotted it is, which is also an indicator of biological activity.

Compost commonly counts on two basic types of organisms to complete its cycle of decomposition. In the early stages of decomposition, a group of organisms know as *thermophyllic* begin the process and generate a great deal of heat as they work their magic. After these organisms have done their job, most of them die to make way for microbes that are more active in cooler temperatures. The organisms are called *mesophyllic*. Mesophyllic organisms work in normal outside temperatures and bring compost to the next phase of completeness. Then, larger organisms such as mites, springtails, and earthworms finish the job.

Mulches do not normally generate the high temperatures that composts do. Mesophyllic microbes, along with larger organisms, do most of the decomposition work in a kind of "cool decomposition" process. Mulches also harbor a variety of insects and other animals that assist in the gradual breakdown of the organic matter and integration into the soil ecology. The life cycles of these insects and other organisms add to the overall biological diversity of the mulch layer, making it one of the richest and most efficient ways to make humus. This is truly the way nature feeds the soil, and why mulches are so effective at improving soil quality.

It is also known that as biological organisms metabolize food and go along their merry lives, they generate heat in the form of calories, just like we do. This tiny bit of heat that is generated by mesophyllic organisms is one of the ways that nature protects tender plants and seeds from the cold of winter. The heat generated by the decomposition of organic matter is also one of the reasons why farmers and gardeners have found natural materials to be such good insulators from severe winter cold for their tender plants. Many natural gardeners who live in climates where winters are really cold mulch their roses and other tender plants with hay, pine needles, piles of leaves, and other organic materials. These materials generate tiny amounts of heat while they slowly decompose. This protects plants above and beyond the physical protection of a pile of material. When there is no more threat of frost, these gardeners pull down the piles that protected their plants and either spread the materials over the soil as mulch or send it to the compost heap to speed up the completion of the decomposition process. They then return this organic matter to the garden in order to sustain the ecosystem of beneficial organisms that keep their soil feeding their plants.

How Compost Is Made

There are several schools of thought on the best way to make compost. I have no particular opinion as long as the end result goes into the soil to improve its quality and ability to support healthy plant growth. I don't care if a compost heap has to sit for a year or if it is finished in a couple of weeks. There just never seems to be enough of it!

I am a fan of fast composting or "hot composting" because I am constantly in need of more compost. So I like to use what is commonly called a "layer cake" compost heap. This layer cake is a series of what are called "browns" and "greens," with a little garden soil mixed in to supply a fresh colony of organisms to new compost heaps. Let's take a brief look at these ingredients.

Compost is a miracle. It is the combination of two primary fuels and biology in the presence of oxygen. This is known as *aerobic composting,* or *composting in the presence of oxygen.* The two basic fuels are carbon and nitrogen. These two basic building blocks of life feed the biological processes that result in the formation of compost.

Carbon is supplied to the process in the form of dried or "brown" material that can be anything from fall leaves to stems. The smaller the brown material particles, the faster they are digested into compost. Brown materials are important because they are the primary structural components that give compost its texture. Browns also feed mesophyllic organisms and thermophyllic microbes with a longer-lasting food source.

Nitrogen is the rocket fuel in the compost heap. Nitrogen-rich materials include freshly cut grass, fresh weeds, and kitchen scraps. These "green" materials promote the growth and proliferation of the thermophyllic organisms that are the first major group of biological critters that decompose the organic matter. A compost pile with lots of green materials will inevitably be hotter than a compost pile that is primarily made up of carbon-rich brown materials.

A little bit of soil from the garden inoculates this combination of greens and browns with the microbes that will do all the work. The soil is not absolutely necessary, but it does speed up the process of microbe colonization. The faster I can get my hands on more compost, the better.

The layer-cake way of making compost is basically a four- to eight-inch layer of brown material and a two- to three-inch layer of fresh, green material with a little soil sprinkled over the top. This layering is continued until the pile ends up no higher than four feet. This height requirement is strictly for management reasons, but it also appears that oxygen circulates better throughout a compost heap that is not too tall. The presence of oxygen is critical for aerobic composting. When oxygen becomes less available, anaerobic organisms (survival without oxygen) begin to colonize the compost heap, and decomposition changes to fermentation. This is when offensive odors are often encountered in poorly maintained compost heaps. Anaerobic fermentation is another way to make compost, but you may end up getting kicked out of your neighborhood for stinking up the joint.

There are countless other ways to make compost and an endless variety of compost bins, drums, cages, and other bizarre contraptions sold as compost makers. I like the good old pile heaped up in the garden. It reminds me of the black gold I'll be using in a few weeks. I often cover my compost piles with a layer of hay so that it is not unsightly. But there is one very important part of making good compost we haven't discussed yet—WATER!

A compost heap cannot function without water. Keep it moist, and moisten it as you construct it so that water completely soaks into the organic matter. Dry material doesn't decompose very well or very quickly for that matter. So keep it moist, and your compost will always turn out perfect.

Benefits of Compost to the Soil

We have briefly talked about how compost promotes soil improvement. Now let's really give it some of our attention.

Compost does some amazing things to soil. It makes no difference what kind of mineral soils inhabit your garden spaces; compost will make your soil a better place for plants to grow.

In clay soils and in silty soils, compost makes soil particles larger and allows for better penetration of water and air. As compost transforms into humus, it also breaks up compacted soils of these two types by allowing earthworms to have a food source. The compost feeds the earthworms, the earthworms burrow in the soil, and the soil becomes more friable due to the integration of organic matter into the soil. Earthworms are only one way that soil structure is improved by compost. Clay and silty soils are actually transformed by the addition of organic matter into loamier material via electrical changes that occur due to optimized ion exchange rates enhanced by the addition of compost. Soil particles that once were magnetically bound to each other become freed from one another, creating a looser soil.

In loamy soils, compost adds to and sustains the organic matter content while feeding the active biology in the soil. Compost has a little less work to do in soils of this type, but does maintain their fertility. This is the heart of sustaining quality soils and one of the areas where compost is so effective.

Sandy soils are one of the soil types where compost really does neat things. The water-holding capability of compost and of the humus it makes creates greater retention of moisture and nutrients. What this means to the gardener is that less water and fewer feedings are necessary to sustain healthy plant growth. Compost fills the large pore spaces between sandy soil particles with organic matter, and a continual supply of organic matter will eventually transform beach sand into a productive garden soil.

The Making of Humus

Humus is the final stage of the decomposition of organic matter and is a very stable particle. It is a spongy material with good water-holding capacity, and it also has the ability to hold dissolved nutrients. We're going to do a little science here.

The makeup of humus is modified from original plant tissue (organic matter) or synthesized by various soil organisms and is resistant to further microbial decomposition. The microbial biomass (soil biology) is greatest in soils receiving continual applications of bioactive organic materials such as compost, organic mulches, and manures. This elevates the overall carbon content in soils, which is the primary elemental component of humus.

Humus has properties distinctly different from the original plant tissue and has its own molecular identity as a natural substance. Some of the properties exhibited by soil humus, which are well known and important from the viewpoint of soil fertility management, include the following:

- Humus particles become bonded to clay and other silicate surfaces (soil particles), leading to the formation of clay-humus complexes.
- Humus stores and releases soil nitrogen.
- Humus possesses pH-buffering capacity.
- Humus possesses cation exchange capacity.
- Humus possesses anion exchange capacity.
- Humus has a filtering effect on contaminants in soils.

Humus is the element of natural soil fertility formation that Justus Von Leibig forgot about in his excitement over the discovery of synthetic plant foods. It is also the most basic element of successful natural gardening. The continual making of soil humus is how natural gardeners grow healthy plants. When we talk about composts and organic mulches, natural fertilizers, and soil ecology, we are really talking about making more humus. It took Leibig his whole life to remember that without humus, soils become sewers. Natural gardeners know that humus is what keeps our soil clean and alive.

Beneficial Microbes and Their Role in Soil and Plant Health

No discussion of soil is complete without touching on the role that some specific beneficial organisms play in soil and plant health. We will focus on specific fungi that are so essential to plant health that without it many plants cannot even survive. These fungi are called

Mycorrhizae (MY-co-rye-zay). Mycorrhizae are parasitic fungi that attach to plants and enhance the plant's ability to find water in drought conditions, reach sources of nutrients, and resist stress. When mycorrhizae establish a relationship with a particular plant, they then reach out into the soil with a massive net of rootlike *hyphae* (hy-PHAY). The hyphae are capable of extracting water and nutrition out of soil many times more efficiently than the roots of a plant can by themselves. This is why mycorrhizal fungi and plants have what is called a *symbiotic relationship.* The plant serves the fungi by providing it with a host, and the mycorrhizae provide the plant with the enhanced capacity to locate and utilize water and essential nutritional substances.

Mycorrhizae are just one family of beneficial microorganisms whose health is enhanced by good soil management. Many billions of other beneficial soil organisms depend on natural gardeners to continue to provide food to them in the form of organic matter. Once a reliable supply of organic matter has been established, these microbes begin to ensure that your garden will be the envy of all who see it—naturally!

Water Conservation and Runoff Prevention

Water conservation and the prevention of water runoff from the garden are two ways that natural gardeners save money on water consumption and fertilizer costs, while protecting their local environment.

Remember that the addition of organic matter to soils increases the water-holding capacity of soils while improving percolation of water through the soil. This prevents and sometimes actually eliminates the loss of valuable and expensive water resources from the garden in the form of runoff. When runoff water is eliminated, so are the nutrients that water carries with it. This prevents nutrient-enriched runoff water from entering into the storm drain system and polluting your local lakes, streams, rivers, and oceans. The prevention of nutrients from running off of the garden also means that they remain in your garden to feed your plants longer. Your garden becomes much more efficient at using the water and the nutrients it receives, while conserving the natural beauty of your local wetlands and aquatic ecosystems.

From the information in this chapter, it is rather clear that adding and maintaining the supply of organic matter to our garden soils is exactly how nature intended us to look after our gardens.

Chapter Four

OUR RELATIONSHIP WITH PLANTS AND WHY THEY GROW

The Sun

The sun is one of the key factors in how plant life got started on this planet. It is also a very integral ingredient in the lives of a much more recent species: humans.

Plants use the light radiated from the sun to convert a complex array of elements into sugars, proteins, carbohydrates, and life via a process known as *photosynthesis*. I hope to explain a little about how this process works in order to make the animal/plant interaction clearer to the uninitiated. Let's start at the beginning.

A very long time ago on a world now called Earth, some tiny bacteria learned to use light from the sun to generate energy. There may have been more than one way to do it, but this bacterium, which was to influence the whole history of Earth, used light upon a green pigment known now as *chlorophyll* to break down carbon dioxide gas into two parts: carbon for its nourishment and growth; and oxygen. The oxygen was released into the atmosphere as a by-product—by far the most precious waste material ever known. This process is now known as *photosynthesis*. It is the engine that energizes and powers all green plants.

We can see the importance of light from the effects of its deprivation. We have witnessed how pale the color and how spindly the growth of plants is when no light is available. Green plants soon die from starvation when deprived of sunlight. An amusing argument against this comes from the infamous author of *Animal Farm*, George Orwell, who describes the Cast Iron plant (*Aspidistra elatior*) and his efforts to kill this plant in his suburban tale "Keep the Aspidistra Flying." All methods proved futile, no matter how cruel; even stubbing out cigarettes in its pot only stimulated it to put out more leaves. The truth is that this plant is an astonishingly efficient light gatherer.

"The force that through the green fuse drives the flower," wrote Dylan Thomas, perfectly describing photosynthesis as the force that fuels plants. The vital chlorophyll molecules are arranged in plates inside these early plants to maximize their efficiency. Kind of like solar panels. Wouldn't it have been weird if chlorophyll had turned out to be a different color than green? We would have been reading poems about the "red, red grass of home"; or watched a movie called *How Blue Is Your Valley*.

But for whatever brilliant reason, the color turned out to be green. Wherever light penetrated, photosynthesizing life could survive. Cyanobacteria (blue-green algae) was the first of these miracle workers. The atmosphere was rich in carbon dioxide, and there was an ample supply of the other minerals needed to sustain life (remember Chapter 2)? As these early plant cells divided—simply split in two, and in two again and again—tiny puffs of oxygen were released. These plants are our first fossil records in rocks known to be over three billion years old and possibly as old as three and a half billion years old.

Let me say that again: Three and a half billion years ago, the first plants began to inhabit this planet. First, imagine each cell exhaling minute amounts of oxygen, maybe enough to fill a balloon the size of a pinhead. Then imagine a world thick with such cells, billions of them, dividing and dividing again, and each time they divide another puff of oxygen is given to the air. Then imagine this process continuing for hundreds of billions of generations. And with each generation, a thousand billion tiny balloon puffs of oxygen are released.

Then the environment attempted to remove the oxygen as fast as it was formed. The natural world loves such reactions. Limestone rocks captured oxygen in the form of calcium carbonates (lime). Minerals oxidized, in the process of gobbling up oxygen into iron ores or rust. Oxygen can combine with so many elements that there are myriad ways to sequester it. And against this reaction, only the tiny cyanobacteria a few thousandths of a millimeter across—puffed and puffed its breath into the New World.

The early atmosphere was very different from the one we know and breathe today. It would be hostile to most life on Earth today. By these slow puffs and the process of photosynthesis, the early atmosphere was modified. Puff by puff, oxygen was added, and carbon dioxide was reduced. It was the life processes of these organisms that shaped our atmosphere and paved the way for more advanced organisms. These early cyanobacteria were simple, single cells lacking both a nucleus and the ability to cohere to larger bodies.

This was also the time when the face of the world was sculpted. The Earth's crust had long since solidified, but the surface of the planet would have carried no recognizable traces of the continents we know today. The earliest continents were probably small and temporary (microcontinents) separated by ocean basins filled with geothermal vents, where all of the heat-loving bacteria could thrive. Volcanic islands rose above the early seas, belching sulfurous smoke filled with more carbon dioxide. The hot springs that bubbled from their flanks were living stews, where simple life used simple atoms for uncomplicated propagation. In cooler pools—where clear water transmitted life—giving light or even between grains of sand on shores, the cyanobacteria lived their brief but momentous existence. They are immortal in the sense that some dim chain of division links these early cells with those that still go about their mindless fission in rock pools around the Hawaiian Islands today.

Sorry to wax poetic about how plants are actually responsible for our own lives, but the miracle of the natural world is so fascinating and important to understanding our interaction with plants that I couldn't help it. The sun is a force that spawned plant life on this planet, and the oxygen we breathe is because of these early plants puffing away and continuing their puffs today. It is these stories of early life that make me grateful that plants exist. That and the fact that I just love mangoes makes me think that plants are very complex and interesting creatures due some gratitude. That gratitude and ten bucks gets me a Caesar salad.

Water

In the present system, plants transmit nutrients in a fluid solution primarily consisting of water. This is true of most of the living organisms on this planet. Proper hydration is important to plants just as it is for humans.

Water is the highway that all nutrients travel on in plants. Without it, few organisms would survive on Earth. It is the universal solvent that puts minerals and other nutrients into solution so that they can be transported from place to place within a plant's tissues.

Proper irrigation of plants is of the utmost importance to their overall vigor. Plants in water stress quickly begin to die as tissues lose their ability to move important nutrients. Some plants that live in arid climates have ways of dealing with drought, but they still require some water to sustain life.

One of the most common mistakes made by gardeners is overwatering. This is just as bad for plants as depriving them of water unless the plants are aquatic and have evolved to live in environments where water is abundant. When plants are overwatered, a number of bad things happen. First of all, overwatering fills the pore spaces in soils with water, and if percolation or drainage is poor, no air can enter into the water-filled pores. When this happens, plants actually begin to drown. Another bad thing that occurs is that waterlogged tissue begins to decay. Without proper infiltration of air, anaerobic organisms begin to ferment the plant tissue and form hydrogen sulfide gas, which is that rotten egg smell you often encounter when digging in waterlogged soils. This anaerobic environment is also a prime environment for pathogenic organisms to proliferate, often resulting in diseases entering and attacking stressed plants.

Natural gardening techniques promote the addition of water-holding organic matter into soils in order to assist in the balancing of the air-water-soil solids dynamic. The accepted balance of components in soil is about an equal division between solids (minerals and organic matter) and pore space. The pore space should contain equally divided amounts of water and air. In optimum conditions, air and water are divided at 25% each of soil components, 45% minerals, and 5% organic matter. This fragile balance is not difficult to maintain in natural gardens because organic matter is such an effective sponge for excess water. So soils that are naturally tended and are rich in organic matter are harder to overwater as well, as they are better at conserving during drought.

Today, many gardens have automatic irrigation systems that provide water to plants without much effort. These sprinkler systems perform a valuable and time-saving service to gardeners. However, irrigation systems have a tendency to put a lot of water out in a short period of time, making it difficult for soils without ample organic matter to absorb moisture as quickly as the sprinklers put it out. This is another way that organic matter helps. When large amounts of water are put down on the garden in a short period of time, the organic matter in soil in the form of compost or on top of the soil as mulch will expand while absorbing the excess water like a sponge.

In the last few decades, irrigation efficiency has improved greatly. With the advent of electronic rain monitors, soil moisture meters that tell an irrigation system when not to water, improved controls and valves, low gallonage, as well as drip irrigation water delivery equipment, wasted water has been drastically reduced. Natural gardeners in the old days did not have this kind of technology at their disposal. In some of the more advanced irrigation systems I have seen in friends' natural gardens, no water is ever lost from the garden unless monsoon rains fall. In your area, you may get these heavy rains, but suffice it to say that if you mulched, the loss of water would be significantly reduced. We don't get many monsoons here in Southern California; in fact, we don't get much rain at all. Those of you who garden in arid climates should consider taking advantage of some of these low-gallonage irrigation systems to save water. Those of you with lots of rainfall can certainly take advantage of the modern electronic devices that shut your sprinklers off during rainy times to save precious water—and even more precious money.

The overall purpose of watering the garden is to give plants exactly enough water to survive and prosper. This is why nature puts cacti in the desert and bananas in the tropics. We gardeners frequently like to grow plants other than those that are native to our climates, and while that may not be the smartest thing to do, we do it anyway. We can grow bananas where I live (in Southern California), but there is no way that banana plants could survive on the amount of rainfall we receive. This is one of the reasons why natural gardeners in my area use loads and loads of compost and mulch to help their soils hold on to moisture and protect the soil from the drying Santa Ana winds and our frequently intense sunshine. The use of these organic materials gives us poor dirt-scratching fools an opportunity to grow exotic plants while maximizing the efficiency of our water use.

The CO_2-O_2 Cycle

Animals and plants have an amazing symbiotic treaty that was forged long before humans, or the plants we're familiar with, inhabited Earth. This symbiosis is how we oxygen breathers get our oxygen supply. The supply of oxygen we continually receive is thanks to every plant on the planet—not just trees or broccoli, but seaweed, marine and aquatic plants, fungi, algae, orchids, roses, and cacti. Some of these plants may not be our favorite creatures, but they are certainly responsible for a part of our oxygen supply.

Conversely, plants have us animals to thank for their supply of the carbon dioxide they inhale. All of the animals on this planet exhale the exact material plants require to sustain their lives. Unfortunately, we build factories and cut down trees, so plants have a larger burden of carbon dioxide to process due to auto exhaust and factory emissions. Here's a good one. Since we have evolved and our taste in foods has included domestic beef, there is actually someone out there measuring how much greenhouse gas is caused by bovine flatulence. Yup, you may run into a person that counts cow farts at your next cocktail party. Plants are overburdened and disappearing at the same time. I am not qualified to make an accurate assessment of this dilemma, but I think it is safe to say that if the oxygen producers leave, so does the oxygen.

Natural gardeners are very smart people because they like to play in oxygen-enriched places—their gardens. Keeping up your oxygen supply is easy—plant a garden. Or just grow a plant or two on a windowsill or out on the balcony. Any plant adds to your supply of oxygen, so I recommend that you grow one. I really like to plant at least one tree a year in a public space somewhere, and I have been known to go out on midnight wildflower seed-sowing raids on the local roadsides in my areas. I really get a kick out of seeing a bunch of California poppies growing in the spring—right where I did a drive-by seeding a few months before.

So, plant something—your lungs will be grateful.

Greenhouse Gases, Global Warming, and Our Oxygen Supply

It's a lot of fun to make jokes about things that are scary. And the present state of our global environment is a very frightening topic, but an important one when discussing the philosophy of why we natural gardeners are compelled to a stewardship of the land without using synthetic materials. Although we garden naturally to produce pesticide- and chemical residue-free plants and food, there is certainly an undeniable environmental aspect to natural gardening.

Today we burn huge amounts of fossil fuels to generate power so we can get from place to place, be warm or cool, light the dark, and manufacture the conveniences of a modern society. These things are now a part of our existence, and it is not likely that anyone is going to choose to go back to the time before computers and disposable diapers in order to save the environment. That whole "back to nature" sect of our society is great if you choose to go there, but I kind of like all of the modern conveniences. I like e-mail, I like my desk lamp, and I like to go fishing on my motorboat. I'm not going to stop driving my car, nor am I about to boycott plastics. I can do a few things, however, that lessen the footprint of my existence on the environment. I am a big believer in recycling stuff. I find all kinds of secondary uses for packages that things come in, and I have learned that there are thousands of alternative uses for newspapers. This is a very small way to preserve some of the resources our world provides me. I don't march in protest of disposable razors, but I do send all of my kitchen scraps to the compost pile instead of to the trash can.

The Machine Age has provided us with oodles of very cool things that make our lives easier. There is no denying that the laptop computer this book is written on is infinitely more efficient than engraving stone tablets. I'm not giving up my computer, and I'm sure that none of you are either. We have fringe groups on all sides of the political issues of life choices. The environmental issue is a classic example of extremism. I don't chain myself to trees, but I also don't think we should be ruining the habitat of endangered or threatened species of plants and animals. I use gas in my car, but I'm not overly excited about drunken sailors ramming oil tankers into pristine, rocky coastlines either. I use my limited sensibilities when dealing with environmental issues and select the things I can change that fit my lifestyle. Then I do them. I choose to tend to my garden without resorting to the use of "rescue chemicals" to make it grow and keep it free of pests and diseases. This I can do willingly, even enthusiastically, in order to have a fractionally cleaner local environment. The more people who choose to do this, the cleaner the entire environment becomes. It's kind of like an epidemic of a good thing, instead of all of the other epidemics we're used to these days.

The burning of fossil fuels increases the amount of carbon dioxide and sulfur in the air. Other molecular pollutants are also released as well. When these materials reach a certain concentration, it creates a situation where certain types of solar radiation remain in our atmosphere, thus heating it slowly. In extremely simplistic terms, this is what is known as the *greenhouse effect*. Remember that person who counts cow farts? Well, those are greenhouse gases as well. Although I'm not sure how the math works in counting bovine flatulence, I am somewhat concerned that the organisms that convert many of the waste materials we produce are not so slowly being reduced in number.

When rain falls through the air these days, it picks up some of these pollutants and falls back to the ground. And while rain is a very good thing, acid rain is not. The deposition of acidic compounds back onto the soil has caused some pretty heavy-duty environmental difficulties for us. Acid rain is one of the most recognized ways that acidic compounds are deposited into the environment. They are directly linked to the burning of oil, coal, and other organic materials. In fact, when the world was young, things such as volcanic eruptions, grassland fires, or forest fires were some of ways our environment became able to support our lives. Carbon dioxide is not a bad material in moderation. Sulfur is not a bad thing in the amounts the environment is able to use. It's when too many of the compounds are available in the natural ecology that problems occur.

Because of acid rain, the Black Forest in western Germany is a mess, and the myriad species that once lived there have been eliminated in favor of a few stressed-out trees and a few plants and animals that are more acid tolerant than other native organisms. Canada and our own country have some pretty serious acid rain issues, too. The former Soviet Union is a disaster area of dead forests, desolate grasslands, and nuclear waste. These things all seem so large and impossible to fix. They are big, but we're working on fixing them. And we natural gardeners are on the back burner of the environmental movement, fixing our own personal spaces. The more of us that there are, the more spaces there are that aren't broken. I like the thought of that.

In acidic soil environments, certain toxic materials that occur naturally (such as lead) become more mobile. Other elements that are naturally occurring that can be toxic become more mobile in these acidified conditions as well. We can use lime and other calcium materials to temporarily counteract these problems, but acid rain and excesses of carbon dioxide will not go down unless we do one thing: Plant more plants! Remember those little puffs of oxygen? That is how nature did it four billion years ago. If each one of us planted one more tree, think of the added oxygen and the reduced carbon dioxide in our neighborhoods. I don't know if it would make us smarter because of the increased oxygen, but we'd *feel* that way.

Agriculture has taken carbon dioxide very seriously, and a relatively new type of farming has taken hold in many areas. This technique of crop production is called *no-till*. No-till agriculture employs a variety of equipment and practices that does not include the plowing or tilling of the land. Large amounts of carbon dioxide are released from soils when they are plowed. No-till agriculture actually sequesters carbon dioxide in the soil instead of releasing into the atmosphere. This is good for plants and for our environment. Conventional no-till systems still employ the use of chemical herbicides and insecticides, but it is a step in the right direction. A few more steps and the no-tillers will be using natural techniques as well.

There are some very good farmers out there using no-till and chemical-free natural practices. It will catch on. The United States Department of Agriculture has recognized the value that no-till cropping systems have in preserving the environment and have begun talks on giving farmers what they are calling credits for carbon sequestration. This program will reward farmers for holding carbon dioxide in their soils instead of releasing it into the air. It is rare when the government does something we can be proud of, but in this case, it appears that our legislators are using their heads.

Chapter Five

CHEMICAL-FREE VEGETABLES

Have you ever gone out into your vegetable garden and just started eating the food right off of the plant? I love doing this. Nothing else seems to matter much when there is a huge crop of ripe snow peas sitting on the plants ready to eat. Few things on this planet are more rewarding than growing one's own food, unless you grow that food without chemical residues on them.

Healthy Food from the Garden

It is no secret that the healthiest way to eat vegetables is to pick and eat them when they're fresh. It is also no secret that vegetables free of chemical toxins are better for us than those that have them. I have never met anybody who preferred to eat foods that were bad for them over the same foods that were good for them. A carrot grown in a natural garden is better for you than a carrot treated with pesticides. Although we eat vegetables for taste, don't we eat them for our health as well?

Earlier we discussed minerals in soils. This is one of the places where the mineral abundance in our garden soil is very important.

When soil minerals are in good supply with respect to the plants growing in them, the plants are able to grow better. The other thing they are able to do is make better proteins and sugars. This translates to more available nutrition for those consuming the plants. The old saying about healthy plants and pest resistance also goes for those who *eat* the plants. Grow healthy plants, and you'll be growing healthy foods.

Without going into a whole bunch of plant pathology and science-speak, we should briefly discuss how natural gardening makes healthier food. Besides the obvious absence of chemical residues, vegetables grown in natural gardens are healthier for us for a number of reasons—the first one being the presence of abundant minerals in foods grown in soils where those same minerals are also abundant. It is a good thing to remember that soil conditions in natural gardens have a propensity to release minerals to plants more efficiently; and because there are so many plant residues in the form of composts, mulches, and fertilizers, the mineral content is better sustained. The result is certainly healthier food that is more consistently rich in essential vitamins and minerals.

Pesticide Residues in Foods

Obviously, natural gardeners don't have this problem. It is, however, a huge problem in food production and consumption all over the world. Remember the apple scare a few years ago when it was found that produce packers were coating our food with a toxic substance called *alar?*

It is good to keep things like this in mind when choosing foods for our families. Even if we were to consent to harmful materials being put on our food, we would never allow it to be a part of the diet of our children or any other loved one. This simple fact is one of the reasons so many of us have chosen to grow our own food: control. When we grow foods in large gardens, small yards, or in containers, we are in control of what substances are applied to those plants. In vegetable gardening, this puts us in charge of the substances that are applied to our food. When we garden naturally, our food is free of residues that may have a negative effect on our long-term health.

In Asia, there is a race of people known as the Hunzas who live very long lives and have little problem with the diseases and illnesses that seem to plague our modern society. They eat foods not dissimilar to our own, but there are no pesticides at all in them. Yes, it's true that the Hunzas also don't eat at McDonalds, but I think you get the picture. No chemical residues means no chemical residues.

Simple Garden Plots

It is often said by people who wish to grow vegetables that they just don't have the room for a veggie garden. I figure that if you have sunshine, air, water, and a patch of dirt, you can have a garden. Size doesn't matter when it comes to growing vegetables. Yes, it is nice to see those perfect half-acre vegetable gardens, and they are very beautiful and interesting places. However, who has that kind of space? It's okay to admire a giant vegetable garden on television and wax romantic about having such a thing, and if you have the space, time, and desire, I say go for it.

Most people have limited personal gardening space, and a good portion of that space is devoted to ornamental plants in their landscapes. When space is limited, I say use your imagination; we have no idea how creative we can be unless we try. Vegetable gardens do not need to be orderly and straight. You can grow veggies very easily in a pot with other flowers or mixed in with your flowerbeds as foliage. If you have a spare section of fence that is bare, grow beans or peas. I once visited a local garden where the gardener had mixed in so many vegetable plants with her amazing flowers and shrubs that it looked like the whole thing was totally natural. She had leaf lettuces and spinach mixed in with her pansies to add interesting foliage, and grew bean tipis behind her taller shrubs to add even more height to her garden.

The place was Eden—her personal Eden. One of the things she had done was to use vegetable plants in her displays of potted plants. My favorite was a beautiful potted hydrangea surrounded with carrots. The deep green and delicate foliage of the carrots made it look like she had ferns growing around the hydrangea. It was spectacular. Then she yanked a few carrots out, rinsed them, handed me one, and we continued our walk, munching away. This is what I call *interactive gardening,* with an emphasis on visual and gastronomic gratification.

Vegetable gardening does not take much space. There is a whole organization dedicated to this axiom. They call themselves Square Foot Gardeners and are dedicated to producing lots of vegetables in small spaces. But this is not a new practice. The French and the English have been producing enormous amounts of food in small places for centuries. One of these methods is known as *French-intensive* gardening and will be our first demonstration of growing lots of food in small spaces.

French-intensive gardening is a practice of placing several plants into a small space and constantly harvesting from it. Plants that require lots of space (such as tomatoes) are staked and pruned to minimize their use of valuable space, while other plants, such as lettuces and root vegetables, are crowded together. These conditions require that plants be constantly thinned. The harvest is in the thinning. This type of gardening also rewards those who like to eat tender and sweet young vegetables. The size of this type of garden can be very small, and I have seen gardens as small as five feet by five feet produce enough food to feed a family of three veggie lovers for an entire summer. This type of gardening technique is especially good for those of you who like to eat lots of leafy vegetables and root crops. Preparation of the site for a French-intensive garden is as easy and fun as eating the plants that abound from it.

Choosing a Site for Your French-Intensive Garden

Pick the site where you have some space. It would be best if it were an area of your property that received at least six hours of direct sunlight during the day. Morning sun and late afternoon shade is good in very hot climates, but you can place your garden anywhere in the sun. Choose the size you want your garden to be. It does not have to be square or rectangular and can actually be any shape you desire. I love it when gardeners use space creatively. Your garden can be a border of low-growing leafy and root vegetables dividing your lawn, and a shrub area. In the heat of summer when leafy crops such as lettuce have a tendency to stress, you can create a beautiful vegetable plot underneath a shade tree. It doesn't matter where you place it or what shape it is. After picking a site for the garden, it is time to prepare your soil for vegetable production.

Soil preparation for French-intensive gardening is very simple. A little digging, a soil test, and application of soil conditioners and plant foods is all you need. After your site is chosen, the first thing to do is dig the soil in order to get a sample of it. If your plot is rather large, you can take several samples in order to get an accurate average analysis of your soil.

Soil-testing services are frequently offered by your local nursery but can certainly be obtained from any farm supply store in your area. A complete mineral or nutrient analysis is the type of test you are looking for. If you have trouble finding someone to test your soil, call your county agricultural office and ask for a list of testing labs in your area. If there aren't any, most universities have chemistry departments that can analyze your soil. If a university near you has an agriculture program, they will be able to do an analysis of your soil without any difficulty. The results will be hard to decipher and read. Most laboratories give you the numeric analysis but also provide simple terms such as *low, very low, optimum, high,* and *very high.* This easy-to-follow method of understanding your soil is very important to the overall health of the plants in your garden.

If your soil has optimum levels of magnesium but is low in calcium, you will not want to use a calcium supplement for your garden such as dolomite, which also has magnesium in it. The application rates I gave you for minerals and nutrients gives a range of amounts to use. If your soil is low in a particular material, use less of it than you would if your soil is very low, but try to remain within the parameters given for adding these materials to your soil. The next step in garden preparation is to add these materials and organic matter to your soil.

Digging your soil to incorporate nutrients and organic matter is a matter of choice. It can be done very efficiently by hand, but machines are now available to cultivate soils in gardens of any size.

There are tractors for large plots, roto-tillers for medium-sized gardens, and the newer mini tillers that weigh less than 30 pounds for cultivation of small spaces. Any of these machines can be rented at a local equipment rental store or can be purchased at home centers everywhere. The mini tillers are really convenient and have a number of other uses besides soil cultivation. The one that I have used is called a Mantis tiller and is lightweight and very easy to handle, so anyone can use one comfortably. Once the soil is initially cultivated, it is time to add your nutrients and some organic matter of your choosing. Incorporate these materials into the soil by tilling them in with your shovel or machine, then water the soil thoroughly. If you can wait, this is a good time to let your soil rest for a few days or until the next weekend, when planting is the gardening agenda item.

Planting your garden in the French-intensive way is very straightforward and simple. Get out your rake, and level off the soil. You don't need to spend too much time breaking up clods of soil, but do try to get a somewhat smooth planting surface. Now it is time to add mulch. A two- to three-inch layer of organic mulch is sufficient. Moisten the prepared garden, and start thinking about plants. This is when you can plant your seeds or your transplants in the garden. Keep taller plants toward the back of the garden so they do not interfere with your ability to reach the smaller plants in your plot. It is also a good idea to try and figure out the angle of the sun on your garden, planting the larger or taller plants so they don't shade your other crops too much.

Some of the tips for practicing French-intensive-style gardening are to plant your plants and seeds close together and thin them out as they grow together, instead of spacing them at the optimum distance from each other when they are small. Not only does this give you more food to eat instead of waiting for plant maturity; it also gives you the chance to see if you like eating ultrasweet and tender baby vegetables. The other thing that crowded gardening in the French-intensive way does is keep weeds from taking hold through competition. So you get lots of food and less weeding. The next type of simple garden plot we are going to discuss is the English cottage garden.

The English Cottage Garden

The philosophy of the English cottage garden may appear to be chaotic to some, but there is great wisdom in this kind of gardening technique. Instead of thinking of the English cottage garden as chaos in green, I like to think of it as a clever use of less space in order to achieve a successful garden. English cottage gardening is not for the habitually organized and anally retentive. It will drive you crazy, so look for more sensible gardening endeavors that are less offensive to your neatness urges.

As in the French style, the cottage garden doesn't need a square or rectangular space to be successful. But because of the myriad of material in one of these gardens, you may want to keep a path or two clear so that you can reach your plants without trampling everything. Pick your site in a sunny spot, and get ready for the fun.

Soil preparation of this type of garden is just the same as we discussed in the French method. Test your soil first, and then add all of your soil conditioners. Rake the garden level, and then add your mulch layer. Then it's time to plant your English cottage garden. Planting in the English style is very simple. Put it anywhere, but put it close together. The thing I like about this style of planting a garden is that I can mix plants up in order to achieve an aesthetic goal, along with the desire to satisfy my constant craving for fresh vegetables. In this type of garden, you can mix culinary herbs into your planting scheme and plant flowering plants that you like to see—all interspersed with your vegetables. The harvesting of the crops in your English cottage-style garden is much like the way it is done in the French-style garden. As you harvest and eat the younger vegetables and herbs or cut the flowers, you make more room for other maturing crops. More food and fun in less space—I like that kind of garden.

For those of you with ample gardening space and a desire to use natural gardening practices in a more organized way, here are some tips. First, pick the biggest-size plot that space and your gardening time will allow you to tend to. The bigger the garden you grow, the more flexibility you will have in types and quantity of plants you can raise. Second, try to place the garden close to a reliable water source, such as a hose bib. Dragging a hose to the garden every time you need to water will get old very quickly, so position your garden close to water. If you choose to irrigate your garden with a drip irrigation system or any other type of automatic sprinkler system, go for it. This will save you lots of time watering. Third, if you live in a rural area where bunny rabbits like to eat plants, consider building a fence with a mesh material that will keep Peter Cottontail hopping on someone else's bunny trail. Don't forget a gate big enough for you to comfortably wheel in materials with a cart or wheelbarrow. Fourth, enjoy your garden; try not to bite off more than you can chew when it comes to size. Gardening for food is supposed to be a fun and relaxing hobby, don't turn it into work by attempting to tend to a garden that is larger than your time and interest will withstand. If you turn gardening into a chore, you're missing out on all of the fun.

Large vegetable garden plots should be in simple shapes such as squares, rectangles, or circles. Although this is not a rule, it does make maintenance a little easier. It is simpler to set up rows of crops in this configuration, and it is much more efficient to get your garden cart into and out of a garden where the rows are relatively straight.

In large gardens, there are several ways to set up your growing beds. You can construct detailed raised beds with wood or any other construction material. You can make raised beds by simply mounding your soil in the chosen growing space. Or you can make your garden look like a small-scale farm by "furrowing" the soil into narrow hills and valleys in a series of rows.

Raised beds are just those—growing beds that are higher than the surrounding soil level. Gardening in raised beds does present some conveniences to gardeners with difficulty bending over, and it certainly allows you to keep the garden more organized. Raised beds can also make room for tidy garden pathways between beds. Constructing formal raised beds can be done by marking out the configuration and then constructing a soil retention wall of almost any height and of almost any material. The most common material for raised beds is wood, and the most common height is between 12 and 24 inches tall.

I have seen some incredible raised beds made of brick or masonry materials, and some very creative ones made from things as bizarre as straw-lined abandoned shopping carts or old bed frames. When constructing raised beds out of wood, a gardener should be cautious of the type of wood preservative used to keep the wood from rotting. One building material that should be avoided when constructing raised beds for edible crops is railroad ties. These wooden ties were and are treated with creosote, which is a very toxic substance. In warm weather, the creosote is released into the soil and can damage plants or allow for potentially harmful chemicals to be released into the soil where your edible plants are growing. Many wood preservatives also seep chemicals into the soil, so care should be used when selecting a preservative for your wooden raised beds.

Raised beds constructed of masonry can also seep strong alkalis into the soil, which may severely alter the pH of the soil in your raised growing beds. My particular favorite type of raised bed is one without formal sides. I like this type of raised bed because it allows me to gradually raise the level of the soil in my beds instead of having to import a bunch of soil to fill constructed raised beds. In this way, I am in control of the quality of the soil in my raised beds by gradually building the soil condition I want season after season. I know this could be done in constructed beds as well, but for the first few years, it would be like gardening in a big bathtub. Hey, there's an idea for a raised bed—recycled bathtubs. I also prefer no formal sides on my raised beds because I can grow low-growing herbs such as thyme and oregano on the sloping soil at the edges of the beds. These ground-cover-type herbs stabilize the soil, while they give me great culinary herbs for the kitchen. These herbs also function as companion plants, which we will be covering in a future chapter.

Building the soil in raised beds should be a slow and gradual process that takes advantage of your own compost and years of mulch layering. You will slowly build a perfect growing medium that is capable of supporting and sustaining plant growth without having to deal with the complications encountered by gardeners who grow their plants at ground level.

Furrow-type gardening is a series of rows that look like hills and valleys. It is the oldest form of gardening that we Americans recognize. The furrow is the valley, and the hill is actually the soil generated by digging the furrow. This was accomplished with a hoe in the old days, but these days, we can use power tools to perform this task.

Furrows are where water is applied to this kind of garden. You put the hose in the furrow, let it fill with water, and the soil takes care of the rest through a process called *capillary action*. Put a paper towel on a water spill, and see how the water moves within the fabric of the paper towel—this is capillary action. I find that although the furrow technique is very useful, it is not very work- or time efficient. I seem to spend a lot of time weeding in this garden configuration. Mulching in the furrows to prevent too many weeds also seems to prevent water from getting all the way down the furrow because the mulch seems to soak up all the water.

Garden pathways are another area where the furrow system seems to fall short of efficient. I like to have a garden cart or wheelbarrow handy when I'm working in the garden, and when I'm working in a furrowed garden, I have to walk all the way back to the main aisle of the garden in order to grab a trowel or my pruning shears. In the raised bed system, I can make garden pathways wide enough to accommodate my cart or wheelbarrow, so my tools, compost, and plant foods are right at my side. I can also haul a radio around in my cart so I can listen to the game or listen to my favorite tunes while gardening. I don't think of the furrow system of gardening as a very efficient use of space, either. It seems like there is just too much distance between rows of plants. This system works fine on larger crops such as tomatoes and corn, but for smaller vegetables, it just seems wasteful.

Veggies in Containers

Vegetable gardening in containers is one of the best ways to take full advantage of growing your own food in a small space. It is also a fantastic way to enjoy the creative use of vegetable plants in arrangements with other plants such as ornamentals. Leafy vegetables are wonderful foliage plants, and certain larger vegetables such as peppers are very ornamental and beautiful in their own right. The creativity that this type of vegetable gardening offers is only confined to one's imagination. Containers can be just about anything. I have seen old toilets used as plant containers. And while I don't find a toilet full of strawberries to be all that aesthetically pleasing, it certainly makes a statement. I'm not sure which statement it makes, but it says *something*. I've seen huge concrete urns with ornamental trees planted in them, and spinach placed around the bottom of the pot as a foliage plant. It was beautiful—and tasty, too.

You can use any type of container to garden, but you must be choosy when it comes to the soil that fills the container. Potting soils come in many different mixtures of ingredients, and some are not exactly suitable for vegetable growing. However, any potting soil is better than trying to grow plants in containers filled with garden soil. Never use garden soil when gardening in containers unless it is mixed with lots of compost and some type of large particle material so that drainage is good.

Potting soils are normally just a mixture of an organic material such as peat moss, or some other material that decomposes slowly. Materials such as wood shavings are also used as bulk materials in the manufacturing of potting soils. Sand is also used to add weight to potting soils and ensure that they don't lose volume. The white specks that you see in most of the potting soils you buy are actually a mined material called *perlite*. This material is used to increase drainage and to prevent the potting soil from becoming compacted. There are two other materials that are used for this. They are *vermiculite* (kiln-cooked expanded mica), and *pumice* (a volcanic stone). The quantity of these materials in potting soils affects how slowly or quickly they drain. These materials really don't have very good nutrient- or water-holding capacity, and potting soils with greater amounts of these materials seem to need fertilization more often than potting soils with high quantities of organic matter. I like to mix my own potting soils and will give you some recipes for a couple of my favorites, but I think we should talk a little bit about potting soil weight.

Some potting soils are lighter in weight than others. I like heavier mixes, but I don't move my pots around very much. If you do move your pots around quite a bit, or don't mind feeding and watering your plants frequently, I suggest that you do use a lightweight potting mix. If you are like me and figure that the pot is fine where it is, use a heavier mix. You won't have to spend nearly as much time watering or feeding your potted plants. Some of the mixes I use to grow vegetables are as follows:

Heavy mix for large vegetables
- 50% washed masonry sand
- 40% organic compost
- 10% vermiculite

Heavy mix for general use
- 40% washed masonry sand
- 50% organic compost
- 10% crushed pumice/horticultural pumice

Lightweight mix for vegetables
- 30% washed masonry sand
- 30% organic compost
- 20% sphagnum peat moss
- 20% vermiculite

I like these mixes because they hold water better than the commercial brands, and they hold on to nutrients for longer periods of time as well. If you intend to mix your own potting soils, start with one of these mixes and see if you can improve on them to better suit your needs. If you are not likely to go through the trouble of mixing your own potting soils, my favorite national brand for a heavier mix is a potting soil manufactured by the Rod McClellan Company, called Supersoil. For a lightweight mix, I have had good luck with one made by Whitney Farms, called Uncle Malcolm's. Another national brand that is a very good lightweight potting soil is the one from O.M. Scott and Sons, called Scott's Potting Soil.

Growing vegetable in containers is a fun and convenient way to cultivate your own food. It is rewarding to grow these beautiful, wonderful plants. Anyone who says they have a black thumb should get a small pot and put some radish seeds in it. In less than a month, you'll be harvesting tasty and spicy radishes with beautiful greens. It takes baby steps to make the transition from black to green thumb. Humans are natural nurturers, so nurture a radish (they don't get nearly enough love).

Seasons for Vegetables

Here's the fun part: choosing what kind of veggies to grow in your garden. One of my favorite aspects of planning a new vegetable plot is poring over seed catalogs looking for that special new green bean that will completely cover my fence with tasty treats. Or how about that heirloom tomato variety that is so flavorful that I just want to eat it right off of the plant. A couple of years ago, I discovered a carrot variety called Thumbellina that looks more like a large orange radish than a carrot. I planted a packet of seeds, and those things were so sweet they have never left my garden.

I also love growing bizarre and unusual vegetables. I like to grow things such as *loofahs* (also known as *luffas),* and then give them as gifts to all of the women I know who use them. Loofah is a member of the squash family of plants, and it is very interesting to grow. The first time I gave one to a friend, she thanked me, but gave me an odd look. When she found out that I grew the darn thing, she couldn't believe it, and then the gift took on a whole new meaning. Now it is a bit of an expected thing. Each fall I get about a zillion calls from people I don't even know who want to get a loofah.

Another vegetable that I grow during our mild winter here in Southern California is kohlrabi. This one looks like a huge turnip growing on top of the ground instead of under it. Kohlrabi has an amazing taste, and many of my friends who have tried it are now hooked as well. The great thing about growing vegetables is how many odd and delicious ones there are out there that go untasted when we count on the supermarket for our produce supply.

Seasons for vegetables can be very simple for people who live in areas where winters are relatively severe. You can't grow vegetables outdoors when there is five feet of snow on the ground and it's 40 below zero outside. So you must wait for milder weather and then grow your crops. But there are still seasons when some vegetables do better than others. Those of you who live in milder climates can grow vegetables all year long. There are very specific times when particular veggies do better than others. This knowledge of when certain vegetables grow better than others is truly a way to ensure better success and fewer crop failures in your vegetable garden. We are going to go through a list of vegetable plants that are commonly grown, along with a few of the more obscure varieties, in order to give you the knowledge of seasonal preference and possibly the desire to try a few oddball vegetable varieties.

Arugula

This plant is grown as a type of salad green and is also known as *rocket*. Arugula is very fast growing and prefers cooler weather. It has a very interesting and nutty flavor. Arugula is a great plant for container vegetable gardens.

Asparagus

This is a perennial crop. Asparagus grows during warm weather and then goes dormant during the winter. This is a crop that loves a thick winter mulch and comes back through it every year for many years. Plant asparagus roots in the spring when the bareroot plants become available at your local garden center. Allow them to grow wild for the first year, and feed them with a food rich in nitrogen, with a balanced mineral content.

Beans

Beans are early-season vegetables in colder climates and winter/early spring vegetables in climates with really hot summers and mild winters. Beans are a quick crop, and they grow very fast. One of my favorite gardening projects is to make bean tipis. I take five or six bamboo or wooden stakes six feet or longer and tie them together at one end. I spread out the other ends and plunge them into the ground to construct a tipi. I then plant about four bean seeds where each stake enters the ground. The beans grow up the stakes and fill in to make a great place for kids to hide in the garden. These tipis also make the crop easy to harvest. If your summers are mild or if you live along the coast, you might try to grow beans in the summertime.

Beets

Beets are an interesting crop that can be grown at just about any time of year. They seem to be sweeter when there is a bit of a chill in the air—around harvest time. Beets are a root crop that can be harvested young and tender or old and crusty. Some gardeners in colder climates leave them in the soil for a while after the first frost to ensure higher sugar content. Beets also have very beautiful foliage and can make an incredibly stunning addition to a flower garden or as a foliage plant in the landscape.

Broccoli

This is one of my favorite foods. Broccoli is a member of a very large and diverse family of vegetable plants called *brassicas,* and produces best in milder weather. It is a great spring and fall crop in areas where winters are severe. In milder climates, broccoli is a must for the winter garden. There are several really tasty hybrids of this crop, and I urge you to experiment in order to find the one you like best.

Brussels Sprouts

This plant is a member of the *brassica* family of plants and really loves cooler weather. Brussels sprouts actually produce their crop on the stem of the plant. Little cabbagelike heads form on the stem at the point where the larger leaves attach. It seems that a brief chill in the air actually makes them sweeter and more flavorful.

Cabbage

Cabbage is also a member of the *brassica* family of vegetable plants. It is a cool weather-loving plant and seems to prefer some chill in order to manufacture its full sweetness. Cabbages can get huge, but there are also some very tasty smaller hybrids if you don't have much space but really like cabbage. I like to plant cabbage in the ornamental garden because of its spectacular foliage in blue-green and purple.

Carrot

Carrots grow best in deep, loose soil. They are capable of growing quite well in either cool or hot weather, but they do appreciate a little shade when temperatures climb into the 90s or higher. Carrots come in several types and shapes. Previously I shared a story about Thumbellina carrots. These are considered a "ball" type carrot. The next longer carrot is a Chantenay, and then Nantes is a little longer and narrower. Danvers is fat and long, and the Imperators are the long, skinny carrots of Bugs Bunny fame. One of the other benefits is the beautiful, feathery foliage that carrots possess. Planting a few carrots around the vegetable garden or in the landscape and letting them go to flower is a very effective way to draw beneficial insects into the garden (due to the rich nectar and pollen content of carrot flowers). The flowers are quite lovely as well. Carrots make great companion plants and will be discussed further for that purpose.

Cauliflower

Cauliflower is another member of the *brassica* family of plants. It is a very beautiful plant and is quite lovely in the garden when its white flowers are forming. The practice of *blanching* is often employed when growing cauliflower crops. Blanching is a practice of wrapping the developing flower head with the leaves of the plant. This prevents sunlight from reaching the flower and keeps it white.

There are several hybrids of this type of plant, including a green variety. Cauliflower loves cooler weather and should be considered a spring and fall crop in cold climates and a valuable winter crop where winters are mild.

Celery

Celery is a member of the same family of plants as dill and carrots. Celery prefers cooler weather and should be grown as a spring crop in colder climates. It can be a very good crop for the winter garden in milder climates. Allowing a few celery plants to go to flower in the garden is very effective for luring beneficial insects into the yard.

Corn

Corn is a very tall crop that can also take up a lot of room in the garden. It is definitely a crop for the hottest time of the year. It should also be planted in blocks instead of rows, unless you plant many rows of corn. The reason for this is that corn requires wind to carry pollen in order for the ears to fully develop. The pollen will just blow away if you only plant a single row of corn. Planting corn into the landscape to add height and backdrop is a very striking and tasty way to add some interest to the ornamental garden. When planting corn in the vegetable plot, try to make sure it is located in a spot where it will not cast too much shade on the other plants in the garden.

Cucumber

Cucumbers are a member of a large family of plants that includes melons and squash. They are known as *cucurbits*. They come in several shapes and sizes and can be grown on trellises as vines as well as on the ground. Cucumbers are a summer crop and should be grown when there is absolutely no threat of frost. I love some of the more obscure cucumber varieties. Lemon cucumbers are little, round, yellow, and very sweet types of cucumbers. The Armenian variety is a long, twisted, light-green and fleshy version of this vegetable that is very flavorful and unusual. This one will make a fine conversation piece at the dinner table, and it makes a fantastic cucumber and yogurt salad.

Daikon

This Asian delicacy is actually a huge white radish. It prefers cooler weather but will tolerate some summer heat with a little shade. Daikons are very delicious and unusually flavorful.

Eggplant

This is a member of the same family of vegetables and fruits as tomatoes and peppers. This is another plant that requires very warm weather to set fruit, and really needs an abundance of warm weather to properly develop. Eggplant has really amazing foliage and can be used in the ornamental garden very effectively. This plant really loves full exposure to the hottest sunshine of the day and will produce great numbers of delicious vegetables. The Italian and Japanese varieties of this crop are more flavorful than the traditional varieties. There is also a very peculiar variety of eggplant that looks just like an egg. This one can be a very unusual and surprising to your kids at Eastertime. And when the know-it-all at your next party tells you the chicken came before the egg, you can show him this one and ask him what kind of chicken lays this egg.

Kale

Kale is a leafy member of the *brassica* family that has very attractive foliage. Several ornamental hybrids have become available in the last decade or so that make very interesting additions to the garden or landscape. Kale becomes sweeter if there is a brief frost around harvest time.

Kohlrabi

This member of the *brassica* family is a very unusual and tasty vegetable that prefers a little cooler weather. The red variety is especially bizarre looking and can be served fresh or steamed. This is one of my all-time favorite vegetables outside of the norm.

Lettuce

There are myriad varieties of lettuces, and some of them can tolerate more heat than others. However, most lettuce varieties prefer rather cool weather and should be grown in the spring and fall in colder climates. In milder climates, it is always good to grow lettuce in the winter, spring, and fall. Summer lettuce is easy in a somewhat shady spot. The many varieties of lettuces all have very lush foliage and can be used in flowerbed arrangements. They are also suited very well to container gardening. Harvesting certain leaf lettuces can be done gradually by cutting a few leaves at a time.

Melons

Melons are a large group of plants in the *cucurbit* family of plants. They require very warm weather to produce a good crop of melons. Cantaloupe, watermelon, and honeydew melon are the more common versions of these plants. Some of the Middle Eastern varieties are very tasty, but my all-time favorite is the Casaba melon. This rascal has the most succulent flesh, and boy, is it sweet. Try a few plants next summer and see if you agree. Melons take up a lot of space in the garden and don't do well if shaded. I put developing fruits on a little bed of hay to keep them from contacting the ground directly. I also turn the fruit sometimes so they don't get bleached spots on them. Melons also use a lot of water and are prime candidates for copious amounts of organic mulch over their roots to conserve moisture in the soil.

Onions

Onions are a versatile group of plants in the lily family. This family of plants includes the amazing health promoter, garlic, and several plants that don't produce much of a bulb. These varieties are harvested for their greens (tops). The most famous of these types of onions are chives. Leeks are a very large version of the green onion that are harvested for their lower fleshy portion. Scallions are little onions with big flavor. And there are numerous varieties of the standard bulb onion. Onions like hot weather and can be grown anytime it's warm. Allowing a few onions to bloom in the garden really keeps pests away. Young onion plants and chives are very interesting-looking plants and should be considered valuable ornamentals. Bunching onions and chives are also very good choices for container vegetable gardens as well.

Peas

Peas are members of the family of plants known as *legumes*. We discussed the nitrogen-fixing capabilities of legumes, and peas will also fix nitrogen into the soil. One of the reasons savvy natural gardeners plant peas in the garden during the early spring is because they like it cooler in the same spot where corn or some other nitrogen user will be planted later in the season. This process is called *crop rotation*, and it serves the corn very well. Climbing varieties of peas are also great plants for the tipis that I spoke of when we touched on beans. Kids love these things. Peas can also be very beautiful ornamental plants, and sweet peas are considered to be the most beautiful of the spring flowers. They are a very colorful way to cover an unattractive fence, or they can be used on tipis for ornamental purposes. Daily harvesting of ripe peas encourages them to produce more food for a longer period of time. So you can extend your crop simply by picking more of the food the plant produces. There are many hybrids and varieties of peas, including ones with edible pods. These are my favorites; I love snow peas fresh or lightly steamed. But my favorite way to eat them is while hiding in a large tipi from those who might try to interrupt my gardening time.

Peppers

Peppers are a member of the same family of plants as tomatoes and eggplant. Peppers love hot weather, and the hotter the climate, the better they produce. There are literally hundreds of different kinds of peppers. There are hot ones, sweet ones, and peppers that are just insanely hot. I was once in a restaurant in Texas and witnessed a whole bunch of businessmen taking these little things out of very beautiful antique pillboxes. I asked my associate what the heck these guys were popping. I thought I was in Amsterdam where people openly take drugs or something. He pulled a similar box out of his coat pocket and handed me this tiny pepper. With a bit of a smirk on his face, he told me to eat it. Well, the damned thing just about killed me, and then 24 hours later, I really paid the price.

Peppers can also be very ornamental, and there are several types that are strictly produced for that purpose. Just pick any really sunny spot in the garden, and plant some of your favorite peppers—then you'll see what I mean. They are really very attractive plants with color- ful fruit.

Potatoes

Potatoes are also members of the same family of plants as toma- toes and peppers. The unusual thing about potatoes is that they pro- duce their crop underground in the form of fleshy tubers. Potatoes can handle a little shade and really appreciate somewhat milder tem- peratures than their other family members. There are hundreds of potato varieties in just about every size and color you can imagine.

There are actually blue potatoes. Some varieties are sweeter than others. I urge you to grow potatoes in very loose ground, and definitely try the Yukon Gold hybrid in your search for the perfect one. Save a few of your favorite varieties over the winter in a cool and very dark place. In the spring, cut up the plants with at least two eyes in each segment. Dust the pieces with just a little bit of sulfur or fossilized kelp dust, and plant them. You will have another crop of your favorite potatoes without having to buy more seeds.

Radishes

Give radishes some love—grow some. The radish is one of my favorite plants because I get food in less than a month. Radishes prefer cool weather, and you can have several spring crops of this vegetable before the summer heat sets in, or you can grow them in light shade in the heat of summer. There are a bunch of hybrids in several colors, including an almost black variety that is very unusual and delicious. This is one of the plants that your children can grow that satisfies a short attention span. They can plant seeds one weekend and have something to eat in just a few weeks. This is how I got started as a kid. I couldn't believe that this little plant could give me food so quickly. Then a child's inquisitiveness took over, and I got interested in growing other things. Now it is just an obsession that some of my friends consider a little odd—until I bring them a basket full of fresh food that is chemical free. Then they think it's pretty great for a day or so.

Spinach

I don't know if I watched too many Popeye cartoons when I was a kid or if I was just a strange child, but I've loved spinach for as long as I can remember. Spinach likes cool weather and ample moisture to produce those succulent, green leaves that are full of iron and about a zillion other good things. I grow spinach in the shade during the heat of summer because I just can't get enough of the stuff. Spinach is also a very pleasing foliage plant and can be grown successfully in the landscape for that purpose. It is also a great plant choice for the container gardener.

Squash

I love growing squash. I think it's because it's so prolific. Most squash prefer warmer weather and should be considered a summer crop. There are two basic types of squash. Summer squash are thin-skinned vegetables such as zucchini and crookneck. Most summer squash grow on bushier plants with few vinelike trailers. Winter squash are normally thicker-skinned varieties such as Hubbard and spaghetti. These types of squash are often vining plants that take up lots of garden space. Pumpkins are a variety of winter squash. There are other squash varieties such as gourds that have hard skins and are inedible to most people. I think a summer garden should have at least one or two squash plants growing in it, and the foliage of summer squash varieties is so large and striking that it is a great plant in the landscape in a very sunny spot. There are some very unusual squash family members, such as loofah, that are fun to grow. But nothing beats fresh zucchinis.

Sweet Potatoes

Sweet potatoes are a lot of fun to grow and have a very interesting flavor. This is a very popular food in certain parts of the world and is a strong source of carbohydrates. Sweet potatoes are members of the *morning glory* family of plants and have a very pleasing flower that is great in the landscape. The larger tubers are formed underground just like potatoes. Sweet potatoes should be considered a warm season crop and can take a little afternoon sun in the hottest climates. Sweet potatoes are a tasty and somewhat underappreciated vegetable.

Tomatoes

Tomatoes are one of those pride crops that vegetable gardeners are constantly bragging about. I have listened to countless stories of superlarge tomatoes or of single plants that produced 300 pounds of fruit in a single season. I like to grow odd hybrids in order to find that one variety of tomato that I just can't live without. Over the years, I have found about six varieties that are now in my garden each season. I like to stake my tomato plants to keep the plants more manageable and to keep unwanted pests off of the fruit by keeping the fruit off of the ground. I have tried all kinds of tomato cage contraptions and have really liked some of them, but I always seem to come back to the simple wooden stake. I also prune my tomato plants to keep them from growing all over the place. Tomatoes are to be considered a warm-season crop and really require mild summer temperatures to produce fruit freely. Try a few different varieties of tomatoes each year to find out which hybrids work best for you.

These are just a few of the bazillions of vegetable choices you have for your garden. The Asian vegetables used in Chinese cuisine are beautiful and tasty. There are also some vegetables from Africa that are a bit bizarre but have great flavor. I really like to try new and different plants in the vegetable garden, and I recommend that you try a few of the obscure vegetables from time to time to see if there is a hidden treasure in them. I also suggest that once in a while you plant a vegetable plant for a combination of food and ornamental purposes just to express your creativity and to harvest food from the landscape garden.

Feeding Vegetables Naturally

Feeding your vegetable garden with natural fertilizers and mineral nutrients is a simple and timesaving alternative to the short-lived and potentially harmful chemical plant foods. Natural fertilizers for your vegetable garden last much longer than the chemical types, and they feed the wonderful biological system that works 24 hours a day, 7 days a week, improving the physical structure and the overall fertility of your soil. Feeding can be done as plants are growing or during soil preparation. I am a real fan of applying plant foods at the time of garden preparation and then during growth checking to see if the maturing plants show any signs of nutrient deficiency. I really do like to let the plants tell me what they need.

Fertilization of vegetables is not very complicated and can be done very effectively with some of the commercial blends of natural fertilizers that have begun entering the general gardening marketplace in the last few years. I am a big believer in convenience, and if you're not interested in mixing your own custom fertilizer blends, the commercial brands are normally very good at providing a reliable supply of essential nutrients without the hassle of measuring and mixing sometimes smelly ingredients.

I do mix my own vegetable plant foods and will give you a couple of recipes that will help you grow the very best vegetables on the most vigorous plants. High-quality ingredients are the keys to success with any plant food, just as it is with our foods. If you want to grow good vegetables, feed them good foods. Here are a couple of recipes that are used in the soil-preparation phase of gardening, and a couple that are faster acting and can be applied to growing crops.

Long-lasting Natural Fertilizers for Application at Time of Soil Preparation

Note: *Each of the following recipes is given to you in increments of parts. A part can be a teaspoon or a truckload.*

High nitrogen mix for vegetables

1 part feather meal
2 parts hoof and horn meal
1 part fish meal
2 parts alfalfa meal
2 parts soft rock phosphate
1 part bone meal

1 part Sul-Po-Mag

2 parts fossilized kelp (Kelzyme)

This fertilizer blend will last an entire growing season for slow-maturing crops such as onions, celery, and pumpkins. It is also a rather high-calcium plant food that will provide your tomatoes with an ample supply of this mineral. You apply this fertilizer directly to the soil when cultivating your garden plot before leveling and mulching. I apply this food to the soil at a rate of about 12 cups per 100 square feet of garden space.

High-phosphorus mix for vegetables

2 parts shrimp meal

1 part seabird guano

1 part fish meal

3 parts soft rock phosphate

1 part New Jersey greensand

1 part cottonseed meal

1 part fossilized kelp (Kelzyme)

This is another long-lasting blend that provides added phosphorus to vegetables such as broccoli, cauliflower, cabbage, and summer squash. It is also applied to the soil prior to planting your crop and will continue to feed the crop for the entire season. This one is also very good for beans and peas. Application rate for this fertilizer is around 14 to 16 cups per 100 square feet.

General-purpose long-lasting vegetable food

1 part feather meal

2 parts fish meal

1 part alfalfa meal

1 part cottonseed meal

2 parts bone meal

1 part Sul-Po-Mag

2 parts fossilized kelp (Kelzyme)

This mix is a good one to use for any general vegetable gardening project and feeds your plants for the entire growing season with no trouble. I also use this mix to feed landscape plants and other general garden plants and trees. This is one of those plant foods that I mix up in big batches, so I have some around and handy all year long. I apply this food at varying rates, ranging from 10 to 20 cups per 100 square feet of garden space.

Fast-Acting Natural Fertilizers for Vegetable Gardens

<u>High-nitrogen booster</u>

2 parts bat guano
1 part fish meal
2 parts alfalfa meal
2 parts shrimp meal
1 part bone meal
1 part kelp meal

This blend really works fast and should be followed by a really thorough watering of the entire area that was just fed. It can last as long as three months, but is best if repeated every 60 days or so. This one is very good at reviving slow-growing and stressed plants. Apply this plant food at a rate of 8 cups per 100 square feet of garden space.

<u>High-phosphorus booster</u>

3 parts shrimp meal
1 part seabird guano
2 parts cottonseed meal
3 parts bone meal
2 parts kelp meal

This is a great natural plant food to add to your plant just as the first blossoms appear on tomatoes, peppers, eggplant, squash, peas, and beans. This mix adds all of the minerals and nutrients needed to promote prolific blossom production and fruit set. I apply this material to the garden at rates ranging from 6 to 10 cups per 100 square feet of space. Remember to water!

Fast-acting general-purpose fertilizer

1 part bat guano
2 parts blood meal
2 parts fish meal
2 parts bone meal
2 parts kelp meal

This mix is a good one for just throwing all over the vegetable garden at feeding time. It lasts for about two to three months and really kicks plants into action. I use this blend at rates of 8 to 10 cups per 100 square feet of garden space, and then I water very thoroughly.

As I previously mentioned, if you are inclined to mixing your own plant foods, try some blends of your own using the plant foods section of this book in Chapter 2. Try a few small batches on some individual plants, and see how they work. One thing about natural plant foods is that they often have very subtle fertilizers that do not burn plants when used sensibly. If you are not interested in mixing your own fertilizers, use some of the many specialty and general-purpose natural plant foods available these days at most garden centers, or check the Resources section at the back of this book. Feeding your plants with natural products can benefit your garden in so many ways. It just makes sense to do it the way nature intended.

Chapter Six

NATURAL FRUITS

G rowing fruit crops without the use of synthetic chemical pesticides and plant foods is as rewarding an endeavor as any other
gardening project. Juicy and flavorful fruits that have no chance of
potentially harmful chemical residues on them or in them just seem
to taste better. I think that the abundance of minerals and natural sugars provided to the plants via natural organic matter and natural plant
foods allow fruit trees to reach their full potential. Eating an apricot
that is so sweet and tasty that you can't imagine anything even coming close is the goal of natural gardeners.

In this chapter, we will be discussing some details about fruit
growing that are specific to each of the more commonly grown fruits,
and some of the exotics as well. We will be touching on general care,
feeding, pruning, dormant care, and a few special traits that each type
of fruit tree has. There are some terms that are used when describing
fruit trees that will come in handy when you are buying new trees or
just gabbing with the neighbors about your fruit crop. Let's look at a
few of those definitions.

Compatible Cultivars

This is a description of tree varieties that can successfully cross-pollinate. Good examples of compatible cultivars are Santa Rosa and Satsuma plum trees.

Crotch

This is the angle of emergence of a branch from the trunk of a tree. Crotches are those joints where a branch connects with a larger branch or the main trunk.

Dwarf and Semidwarf Trees

These are terms given to describe fruit trees grafted on to size-controlling rootstocks. Dwarf trees usually reach a height of 8 to 10 feet. Semidwarfs mature at 12 to 18 feet in height.

Genetic Dwarf

These fruit trees have a genetic propensity to stay quite small. They often mature completely at a height of 4 to 5 feet tall.

Graft and Bud Union

A graft or bud union is where the tissue of one type of tree is joined with another. Often the position of the graft or bud union is marked with a pronounced scar. Grafting and budding are methods used to join vigorous rootstocks to fruiting varieties.

High-Chill

High-chill trees require more hours of cold or cool weather the break dormancy. This means that a high-chill tree requires many hours of chilly weather before it will come out of dormancy and begin to grow in the spring. High-chill trees do not perform well in mild climates. Many apples, pears, cherries, and deciduous fruit and nut trees are rated by the number of hours of chill they require.

Low-Chill

Low-chill deciduous fruit trees require fewer hours of cold or cool weather in order to break dormancy. These deciduous fruits and nuts do best where winters are mild.

Pome Fruit

Pome fruits are fruit types that have cores that contain more than one seed. Apples and pears are representatives of the pome fruits.

Rootstock

A rootstock is normally a very vigorous growing variety of compatible plants that a fruiting variety of plants are grafted onto. Rootstocks are selected for their vigor, or for their capability to keep plants small or dwarfed.

Scaffolds

This is a term used to describe the main or structural branches on a fruit tree—or any tree, for that matter.

Self-Fruitful

Self-fruitful trees are trees that are capable of producing pollen that is able to pollinate its own flowers. Another term for trees of this type is *self-pollinating*.

Spurs

Spurs, when used in describing fruit trees, refer to a type of wood where a majority of the fruit comes from. They are also called *fruiting spurs*. They are short branches that appear to have lots of growth buds on them, giving them a rather knobby appearance. Spurs only grow a few fractions of an inch in length per year. As spurs form on your apple, pear, apricot, or plum, you will recognize them, as this is where most of your spring blossoms will come from. And where the blossoms are, that's where the fruit will be.

Standard

This is a term used to describe full-sized trees. Standard trees usually mature at a height of at least 20 feet.

Stone Fruit

Stone fruits have a single large pit or seed in the middle of the fruit. Peaches, plums, and apricots are examples of stone fruits.

Suckers

Suckers are shoots that sprout out of or near the base of a fruit tree. Suckers are found lower than the graft union and should be removed as soon as they are noticed.

Watersprouts

Watersprouts are upright shoots, often vertical, that sprout from the main branches and trunk of the tree. These are energy users and should be removed each dormant season at the time of pruning.

Whips

This is a name given to young trees or first-year growth from a graft or a bud union. These terms are useful when discussing fruit trees and will come up a few times during this book and in just about every other gardening book that discusses fruit tree care. These words are good ones to know.

One of the wonderful things about growing fruit in the home garden is that since the advent of the dwarf tree, gardeners do not need to have acres of land to cultivate a tantalizing selection. Here in California, land developers and homebuilders carve the tops off of mountains in order to develop more land for home sites. The resulting lots are often quite small, with large sloping sections that have become very popular spots for growing fruit trees. These "slopes" have become major garden space due to the lack of open, level ground on the postage stamp lots where they build the oversized houses we have become so accustomed to. People with the desire to garden have had to move onto these slopes to satisfy their gardening urges. Fruit trees are uniquely suited for this uneven terrain, and if planned nicely, a fruit orchard on a slope can be a very attractive addition to the overall beauty of one's outdoor space.

Natural Care of Fruit Trees

Caring for your fruit tree is mostly a matter of understanding what the plants require and at what time of year they need special attention. In most parts of the country, when the topic of fruit tree care is discussed, it means deciduous trees that lose their leaves during the wintertime and produce fruit during the late spring summer and fall.

However, there are many gardeners who grow evergreen fruit trees in climates where winters are milder. And some of us are lucky enough to be able to grow exotic tropical fruit varieties along with the more common varieties. So we will be discussing care techniques for each basic group of fruit named here. As usual, let's start with the soil.

Fruit trees are not all that particular about soil. Most trees can be grown in any number of mineral soils as long as water application and irrigation match the ability of the soil to percolate. With a good layer of mulch around the base of the tree and out to the dripline to assist in moisture conservation, soil conditions from a standpoint of whether the soil is a clay or a sand makes little difference. Fruit trees find ways to cope with even the most adverse soil conditions as long as you feed them properly and keep organic matter around their roots in the form of mulch. As the mulch decomposes and the soil conditions improve, you will begin to see increased yields and fewer problems with pests and diseases.

I truly think that a four- to six-inch-thick layer of mulch around the tree and directly above the feeder roots can counteract any bad soil conditions that can be thrown at a gardener wishing to grow fruit. One key is to make sure that each year, the mulch layer is supplemented with additional mulch that accommodates the tree's increased size as well. The most important dimension of the mulch ring around a fruit tree is that the mulch goes out about a foot farther than the dripline of the tree. In many cases, I like to see the mulch ring two or three feet out past the dripline of the tree. For those of you who are not familiar with the term *dripline*, I have a very easy way for you to find out where the dripline of any tree is.

If you were to place yourself directly above any tree of any size and draw a circle on the ground that mimicked the outside edge of the tree, that would be the dripline. For instance, if your apricot tree's farthest leaves were eight feet from the trunk of the tree and you were to tie a string to the trunk and give yourself eight feet of string, you should be at the outside edge of the tree. Directly above you would be the farthest-reaching branches, and under your feet would be where your tree takes in most of its food and moisture. If you were to draw a line in the soil at the 8-foot mark and follow that string all the way around the tree making a 16-foot diameter circle, you would have a line where the dripline of your tree is. The trunk is the center point of your circle, and the line you drew in the soil is where you should feed your tree when it comes time for feeding. It is also where you should water your tree when it is time to irrigate, and where you should place mulch under the tree. Remember that where there is organic matter, there is life in the soil. Doesn't it make sense that you would put the greatest amount of nutrient availability and biological activity exactly where the tree can use it most?

I have seen many occasions where fruit trees were fed right up next to the trunk of the tree. There are few, if any, feeder roots that close to the trunk. So it would seem like the fertilizer is wasted, and it is. The very best way to ensure that your fruit trees are superhappy and healthy is to put their food supply close to where they can use it.

A system of placing you feedings where the trees can use them best is now easily done with the invention of the new types of drop spreaders on the market. Gone are those old metal things that rusted after one use. Today you can find very good plastic drop spreaders for around $25 at most home centers. Fill this rascal up with your minerals and plant foods, then just make a couple of circles under the tree every 6 or 12 months or so. It is a lot more precise than feeding the trees by hand, and only takes about a minute or so to feed a fully mature fruit tree this way. Then put your yearly layer of mulch on top of your feeding, and you're done for the year. Taking care of the soil under fruit trees probably takes no more than one hour per year in a natural garden.

The biggest benefit to keeping that mulch layer continually replenished is what it will do to gradually improve your soil. The second best thing a thick layer of mulch does is preventing many weeds from getting a foothold in your fruit orchard. My favorite time of year to mulch the fruit trees is in the late fall after the trees have dropped all of their foliage if they are deciduous trees, in early spring on evergreens, and whenever I think it's getting too thin around tropical fruits. I also like the fact that the mulch layer makes for some great planting areas for annual flower arrangement and companion plantings to add color and insect control to the fruit orchard. Few things are prettier in the garden than a tree full of fruit, with a profusion of colorful flowers blooming under it. The mulch layer makes it all possible and sustainable, while it builds the quality of the soil your trees are living and feeding from.

By beginning this process of soil building as soon as you plant your new trees, you will have improved the soil around your trees significantly by the time they begin to produce fruit. This system will improve the soil in an expanding circle as your tree grows. As the tree reaches maturity, you will have built soil conditions perfect for optimum fruit production, no matter what kind of soil you started out with.

Pruning and Dormant Care

Caring for your deciduous fruit trees during the dormant season is at least as important as how you care for them when they are actively growing. This is the time of year when you can prune your trees to take maximum advantage of fruit-producing wood, while keeping unwanted and dead wood out of the tree. It is also an important time for prevention of insect infestations and for disease prevention. The dormant period for deciduous fruit trees is during the cold part of the year. This is how this type of fruit tree conserves energy and protects itself in times of severe cold. Some deciduous trees are actually daylight sensitive and will begin to go dormant when the days get shorter.

The practices of pruning and dormant season care are somewhat specialized for many varieties of deciduous trees. In this next section, we will discuss some of the significant differences between different varieties of deciduous fruit trees. But first, I think that it might be appropriate to have a brief discussion on fruit tree pruning so we are speaking the same language as our discussion continues on specific types of trees. Here is some general information on pruning that may help you make good decisions when approaching your deciduous fruit tree to prune it.

Fruit Tree Pruning

To ensure the production of high-quality fruits and to improve access to that fruit at the time of harvest, you will need to shape or prune your fruit tree into a sturdy and efficient framework that serves your needs while serving the health of the tree. For smaller orchards or for the home gardener, there are two basic pruning methods that are commonly employed. These two methods are known as the *center leader* and the *open center* methods. These two methods promote the utilization of strong, wide crotches in their branching that are far less likely to split when weighted down with a heavy load of fruit. Doesn't a heavy load of fruit sound nice!

One of the most important and often overlooked pruning practices is to start early in the development of the tree. Planting a young tree and letting it grow wild for three seasons before it is shaped and pruned is not a good way to ensure that your fruit tree will have the shape that you desire. Start the very first season looking for promising branch structure that will allow you to have a tree that is strong and symmetrical. Starting when the tree is young will also give you the opportunity to remove unwanted growth while it is still very small so that when you take it, it does not grossly affect the tree's shape.

When young trees are pruned each year, it is more of a "touch-up" than a drastic removal of unwanted growth that has been on the tree for a few years. Open-center tree pruning is the most commonly used technique for plums, prunes, peaches, nectarines, apricots, and figs. The open-center method keeps the center of the tree clear in order to maximize air circulation and sunlight penetration throughout the branches. Proper air circulation within a tree prevents many of the disease and insect problems related to poor air circulation. The center leader method is very often the technique of choice for pears, apples, and cherries. I also like the open-center technique for cherries and some of the Asian pear varieties. Many apples and pears produce fruiting spurs, which we will touch on later in this chapter. The central leader practice for these trees is very effective for maximizing the production of these fruiting spurs.

When pruning your young trees, try to pick branching crotches that are very wide and more perpendicular to the trunk than angled. Angled and narrow branch crotches have a tendency to produce excess tissue in the crotch of the tree, weakening the crotch and increasing the possibility of a branch splitting or breaking off of the tree. This training of branches is called *spreading* and can be accomplished by placing wedges of wood in the crotch of the tree to spread the branch to a more horizontal plane perpendicular to the trunk. Weighting the branches with something heavy tied to a rope and hung from the branch is another method of spreading. Always remember to protect the bark of the tree from abrasions with old rubber hose sections or bits of cloth wrapped around wood or rope where it contacts the tree. This will prevent wounds in the tree where insect pests or disease organisms might enter the plant. For center leader-configured trees, a stake may prove to be a good guide during early development of the scaffolding. Building a good framework early in the development of your tree will make life easier for you and the tree as it matures.

Knowing *when* to prune your deciduous fruit trees is just as important as *how* you do it. Some trees such as apples and pears can be pruned very early before the trees begin to break dormancy. Other trees such as peaches, plums, and apricots really should be pruned right around the time you see the buds along the branches beginning to swell. Waiting like this cuts down on the chances for infection by diseases. When pruning, always remove crossing branches in favor of the branch that suits the shape of the tree better or has the stronger crotch attachment to the trunk. Remove all dead and decaying wood from the tree. And last but not least, if you live in a climate that gets cold, do not for any reason prune your trees in the fall. This may stimulate a growth spurt that could be damaged by fall frosts. This damage can be very bad for the health of the tree. Now let's look at several of the more common deciduous fruit varieties.

Apples

Just about everyone knows the name of his or her favorite variety of apple. Mine is a sour apple called a Granny Smith. I can't grow Granny Smiths in my climate, however, because it is a relatively high chill variety, and I live in a very low-chill area. Pick an apple variety that fits your climate. Apple trees really need some consideration of space when you choose a spot for them because a standard tree can reach a height of 20 to 30 feet. Some of the dwarf varieties out there get no larger than six feet tall, so choose your plant wisely in consideration of the space you have available.

Most apples begin to develop fruit in the third year after planting. It is wise to discourage your apple tree from fruiting until the third year in order to expend its energy on good growth instead of early fruit production. Apples prefer a sunny spot in the garden and really appreciate good air circulation. When choosing a pruning method for apples, it should be recognized that most professional orchardists choose the center-leader method of training their trees. Prune your apple trees to have a wide-angled branching pattern, and avoid narrow-angled crotches. Prune your trees each year to admit light into the tree and encourage good air circulation. Also, remove dead and diseased wood each year, and get rid of crossing branches in favor of the stronger branches that fit the shape of tree you are attempting to achieve. Remove or thin out some of the branches where dense growth prevents light and air from entering the tree. Most apples produce fruit from spurs, and it is a very good idea to learn to recognize fruiting spurs when you see them.

To encourage stronger growth on spindly branches, prune the end of the branch just above an outward-facing growth bud. Outward-facing growth buds face directly away from the center or trunk of the tree. Some apples are said to be self-fruitful or self-pollinating, but most prefer or require a compatible cultivar planted within 40 or 50 feet for good pollination.

Today you can find apple trees with several varieties of apples that are compatible cultivars grafted onto the same tree. This is a big space saver. These trees are referred to as *four-in-one* or *five-in-one* trees. It depends on how many varieties are grafted onto the tree. I have seen some of these trees, and they appear to be a very good way to get a good selection of apples while ensuring excellent pollination. Apples do require dormant spraying, which we will discuss at the end of this section. Good sanitation of the area under an apple tree will minimize diseases and pest problems, so pick up that fallen fruit. If it is not edible, put it in the compost heap. A mature apple tree in full bloom is one of the most spectacular displays of color in the garden and is a harbinger of spring.

<u>Apricots</u>

Apricots are another variety of deciduous fruit trees where most of the fruit and blossoms appear on spurs. It is a very good idea to give standard apricot trees some room because they can get between 20 and 30 feet tall and just as wide. They prefer a sunny planting site with good air circulation. Most apricots are self-fruitful, yet some varieties produce larger harvests when pollinated by a compatible cultivar. Apricots are pretty hardy in cold winter areas, but it is a very good idea to check and see which are the best varieties for your climate.

When choosing an apricot tree, try to make sure that it is grafted onto seedling apricot stock instead of a peach rootstock. The peach rootstocks don't grow as well, and apricots have some apparent difficulty with dwarfing rootstocks as well. If you need a dwarf tree, try to find a genetic dwarf apricot. Apricots really begin to bear good fruit yields in their fourth or fifth year. When the tree is young, it is a good idea to concentrate on the shape of the tree instead of trying to get an early crop off of it. If you do this, you will be grateful for your patience, I assure you.

The pink blossoms of apricot trees are very lovely, but the tree has a tendency to bloom early in the spring and may suffer the consequences of late frosts. This is another reason to be sure the chill requirements of the trees you choose are compatible with your climate. A high-chill variety is always a safe bet in areas where late spring frosts are commonplace events. Apricots are also notorious for setting way too much fruit. This can result in undersized and off-flavor harvests. Thin out your fruit if it looks like your trees are just too overburdened.

Apricots are also great for drying. When you harvest your fruit, don't forget to break out that Popeil's fruit dehydrator that has been gathering dust for years and dry some apricots. Ron Popeil will be grateful. And you'll get some use out of a moment of infomercial weakness.

Cherries

I love fresh cherries, but since there are no varieties of cherry trees with low enough chill requirements to grow in my area of the country, I can't grow them. I envy gardeners in colder climates who can grow cherries. I have visited parts of the country where cherry trees grow, and I really admire their beauty in bloom. They are spectacular trees, and you get a real treat when it comes time to pick the fruit.

Cherry trees come in two types: sweet cherries, and tart or sour cherries. Sweet cherry trees get a bit larger than sour cherries, reaching heights of 30 feet, while sour cherries top out at about 20 feet tall. Cherries are very chill-sensitive trees, so it's a good idea to make sure that the variety you choose is compatible with your climate. Most sweet cherries require a compatible cultivar for good pollination, but I think that some intrepid nurseries are grafting more than one variety onto a single tree to ensure good pollination for those gardeners with limited orchard space. Most sour cherries are self-fruitful and are also a little hardier in ultracold climates. Sour cherries are hardy to 30 degrees Fahrenheit, while sweet cherries appreciate the milder 20-degree range of temperatures. Heck, it rarely gets below 50 above zero in my area, so you can see my cherry tree dilemma.

Sweet cherry trees should be pruned using the center-leader method and really benefit from wide-crotch scaffolding. Sour cherries have a rather open growth habit and benefit from an open-center pruning technique. Both sour and sweet cherries appreciate a sunny location and very good air circulation. Pruning should be done with a light touch on cherry trees, and removal of crossing branches and dead wood is often enough after you have established a strong and symmetrical scaffolding. Cherries do require dormant spraying to remove the possibility of disease and overwintering, unwanted visitors. Sharing part of the crop with the local bird population can be frustrating, and your trees may require some creative scare tactics. There are several bird-chasing methods, but I like the Mylar foil strips hanging in the tree. I have a friend who put decoy owls in his trees, and it seems to work (although it looks pretty silly).

Nectarines and Peaches

Nectarines and peaches are really the same plant separated by a single gene. I don't know what the scientific name for that gene is, so let's call it "the fuzz gene." Peaches have the fuzz gene, and nectarines don't. Nectarines and peaches are both very chill-specific, so when choosing your tree, you should be aware of getting a variety that will thrive in your climate.

The size of a peach or a nectarine plant can range from 4 feet (genetic dwarf) to 20 feet tall (standard). Both nectarines and peaches love a sunny spot in the garden and prefer the open-center method of pruning. Thinning of fruit is an important part of caring for these trees. Peaches and nectarines are mostly self-fertile, and can bear so much fruit that they will actually break off overburdened branches. Thinning also ensures that your peaches and nectarines reach their full, succulent size. Too many fruit often results in smaller fruit. *Freestone* and *clingstone* is the way these plants are classified.

Freestone fruit separate from the center pit easily, and clingstone fruit hold on to the flesh of the fruit. If you have room for more than one of either of these trees, pick one tree that is an early-ripening variety, and another that ripens later in the year. This will extend your harvest time and keep you in fruit longer. Few things in this life are more rewarding than biting into a fresh nectarine or peach right off of a tree that you have nurtured. Once again, make sure that the variety of either of these trees you choose to grow has the appropriate chill requirements for your area. This is where most failures occur in fruit production and overall vigor of the tree. Whether you prefer the fuzz gene or no fuzz gene, try one of these fruit trees in you garden. Nectarines and peaches are not spectacular bloomers, the way some other deciduous fruit varieties are, but the harvest is hard to top.

Pears

Pear trees produce oodles of sweet and tasty fruit—my favorites among the deciduous fruit varieties. The trees can range from 6 feet to more than 30 feet tall, depending on the cultivar and the rootstock.

Pears have a tendency to grow somewhat upright, and seem to appreciate the center-leader-type pruning method. The European pears such as Bartlett and DeAnjou have been popular for years. But now, Asian varieties shaped more like apples have begun to show up on produce racks. These Asian varieties are very sweet, and the trees are as easy to grow as the stalwart European types.

Asian pears are a little less formal in their growth habits and prefer an open-center pruning style. Pears are very chill selective, and you really need to know if the variety you select is compatible with your climate. Pears are great in the orchard, but are also amazing additions to the ornamental garden. Their white blossoms are very striking and are a sure sign that warmer weather is on the way. They tend to bloom a little later than other deciduous fruit types and are less apt to suffer from early frost damage.

Pears appreciate a sunny spot in the garden where air circulates well. Most of the fruit and blossoms are formed on spurs, so it is a good idea to learn to recognize this type of fruiting wood and maximize it when you prune. European pears have a tendency to be upright growers, and branch crotches will normally require some spreading to strengthen them. Pears ripen in the late summer or fall. Some varieties are considered to be self-fertile, but a compatible cultivar is normally required to assure a good crop of fruit. I think that nurseries are combining fruit types on single trees for this purpose, as they do with apples.

Persimmons

This is not nearly as obscure a fruit as you might think. The Native Americans loved the fruit that came from the persimmons indigenous to North America. The American persimmon has a somewhat astringent flavor and needs to be mushy-ripe to be sweet enough to eat, but boy oh boy, can you make some incredible desserts with this fruit. Asian persimmons are larger and sweeter than the American varieties, and can be eaten sooner. American persimmons are also hardier than their Asian counterparts and can be grown in climates where temperatures get as low as 25 degrees Fahrenheit. Asian persimmons can take temperatures around zero, but they prefer milder climates. Persimmon trees are very ornamental and turn brilliant colors in the fall. They hold on to their fruits long after they lose their leaves, making them somewhat unusual looking. Birds will come from miles around to eat your persimmons, so share a few, or just plant a tree to draw birds into the garden. Persimmons are notorious for sucker production, so a thick layer of mulch is a must around these trees to discourage this behavior.

Plums

Plums are very prolific fruit trees and produce huge crops of supersweet fruit with a little tartness. I eat them right off of my mom's trees with enthusiasm. Plum trees can be found in sizes from 4 feet to 20 feet tall, depending on their rootstock. Plums also bear their fruit on spurs that are easily recognized, and can be used as a learning aid in recognizing fruit spurs on other types of deciduous fruit trees. European plums are hardier than Japanese varieties and can take more severe winter cold. American plums are actually bushes that bear small fruit and are not considered as good table fare as European and Japanese varieties.

Japanese plums prefer an open-center type of pruning and really enjoy good sunlight and air circulation in the center of the tree. The European varieties seem to do best when pruned with a center leader. Dead air or too much shade inside plum trees is a sure-fire way to attract every nasty pest and disease in your county. You're going to share a few with the birds, also, if you don't take steps to deter them. Plum trees prefer a sunny spot in the garden where there is little chance of late frost. Most fruiting plums put on a spectacular show of pure white blossoms in the spring, making them good choices for the ornamental garden as well. There are also several varieties of ornamental plums with different-colored foliage and striking flowers.

These are some of the more popular deciduous types of fruit trees grown in the residential garden. If you have room for an orchard, I suggest that you try as many of these trees as you can. They provide nice spring color, tasty treats, and some of them actually make pretty good shade trees. They do require a little extra care during the dormant season, but the reward overshadows any extra work. One of the ways why gardeners care for their deciduous trees during dormancy is to apply materials that fight off pests and diseases. When the trees are bare, it is much easier to get to all portions of the tree. One of the ways to ensure that your trees remain healthy is to prune them. The other way is to dormant spray. Dormant spraying allows you to apply materials to your trees that will keep your trees free of pests and diseases that may spend the winter hiding there. Let's discuss a few materials used by natural gardeners as dormant sprays.

Dormant Spray Materials

<u>Baking Soda</u>

Sodium bicarbonate or baking soda is a very effective fungicide. It works to protect plants from future disease attacks, and also eradicates some organisms that may already have made a home on your tree. I like to mix about 3 to 5 tablespoons to a gallon of water, and add a little dish soap to help it cling to plant surfaces. This can also be applied during the growing season at half strength.

<u>Bordeaux Mixes</u>

Combining copper sulfate with hydrated lime makes Bordeaux mixes. This material is widely available at garden centers and is one of my favorite dormant sprays. It combines the powerful fungicidal properties of both of these materials, and is also somewhat effective at controlling pest insects as well. I only apply Bordeaux during the dormant season because it can burn foliage, and we should also remember not to use too much copper. It is a trace mineral only used by plants in small amounts.

Citrus Oils

The rind and peels of citrus contain two known pest controllers. Linalool is a nerve toxin to pests and eradicates them on contact. The other material in citrus oils is d-limonene. It is not presently known how d-limonene controls pest populations. The great thing about applying citrus oils is that it smells like oranges and has no toxicity to humans or any residue. Two to five tablespoons of citrus oil in a gallon of water, with a drop or two of dish soap to keep it suspended in the water, makes a very good spray.

Compost Tea

Yup, not only does compost feed your soil, but a tea made from soaking it in water is a very effective fungicide as well. Compost tea can be applied during dormancy or directly on the plant during the growing season. It works by introducing competitive beneficial organisms that fight the bad guys for space or feeding on them directly. Making compost tea is easy. Start with a bucket filled with a gallon of water. Put about a cup full of finished (that's important) compost into a tea bag made of cheesecloth or an old stocking. Soak it in the sun for a few hours, and then apply it to the tree.

Horticultural or Superior Oils

These very pure oils are produced in the manufacture of paraffin waxes. Some superior oils are still refined hydrocarbons. These materials are very effective for smothering overwintering pests and suffocating them. They are also efficient sealers of the open cuts on your trees right after pruning.

Hydrogen Peroxide

Hydrogen peroxide has the same effect on plant wounds as it does on our own cuts and scrapes. I use a little hydrogen peroxide in every dormant spray I mix up. Normally I use between 2 and 5 table-spoons in a gallon of prepared material.

Lime-Sulfur

By adding lime to sulfur, the fungicidal properties of sulfur are enhanced. Lime causes a chemical change that allows sulfur to pene-trate plant tissues. Then sulfur can get at disease spores and eradicate them. This material can be purchased commercially, and precautions should be taken not to apply it in hot weather. Do not apply any sul-fur products to apricots. It will affect the yield, and the fruit will taste sulfuric.

Neem

Neem is more than just an insecticide. It has fungicidal properties as well. Neem can be found at most nurseries and garden centers. It is the oil extracted from the seeds of a tree native to southern Asia.

These materials are very valuable to a gardener attempting to grow fruit trees naturally. Each of these materials occurs in nature, and each is a very effective tool. The key is to know how to use them and how and when to apply them. I like to apply the first dormant spray-ing right after the trees have lost all of their leaves. I then do an addi-tional spraying about two weeks later with another material so the bad guys might have been resistant to my first spray are controlled. I then apply my last spray immediately after I finish pruning. This spray application is to seal the wounds in the tree (made when I pruned), and to prevent any early spring visitors from making their home in my trees. Here is my program; however, I suggest that after some testing, you come up with one that works for you best.

My Spray Program

In the late fall after the leaves have dropped is the time when I like to focus on the insect stragglers and use either a neem product or citrus oils in order to shorten their lives. I might add some hydrogen peroxide and baking soda to this mix if the trees had a bad year, with diseases such as mildew or peach leaf curl. My mixture consists of the following ingredients in a gallon of good old tap water:

4 tablespoons neem extract or neem oil
    or
6 tablespoons citrus oils
$1/4$ teaspoon of dish soap or pure Castile soap

If I'm inclined to, I'll add:

4 tablespoons of regular Arm and Hammer baking soda
2 tablespoons of food-grade hydrogen peroxide, or 6 tablespoons
    of regular hydrogen peroxide off of the drugstore shelf

My second spraying is to target disease, and I just apply good old Bordeaux at the mixture rate suggested on the package in which I bought it.

Then in the early, early spring, I prune my trees and apply the last of my dormant sprays. This material is applied to keep bad guys from entering the tree from the open cuts left during pruning, and to give one last uppercut to any loitering pests. This mix is normally a horticultural or superior oil product applied according to the label on the bottle.

Each time I apply spray materials to the trees, I make sure to cover every bit of it, and then I spray the trunk of the tree and the soil immediately around the trunk. When spring comes, I am confident that I have done all that I can to ensure that a tree begins the growing season free of nasties.

Evergreen Subtropical, and Exotic Fruits

Most evergreen fruit varieties come from milder climates. Here in the USA, we grow most of the evergreen fruits we produce in warmer southern latitudes often called "the citrus belt." This is because the vast majority of evergreen fruit crops grown for our consumption are varieties of citrus. But did you know that in California we have a huge avocado industry? Florida and Texas farmers also grow a lot of avocados. There are also sections of our country where exotic tropical fruits such as bananas, papayas, mangoes, and some very peculiar fruits can be grown.

Gardeners who have five feet of snow on the ground in the winter do not normally grow these types of plants. Yet in the Victorian era, the wealthy gardening enthusiasts had conservatories where they grew some of these more exotic fruiting plants. The often-used term for a conservatory was an *orangerie*. This is where they kept their oranges and other fruit crops that required protection from severe winter cold.

Today we have greenhouses, and we can grow just about anything we want from anywhere in the world in one of them. Subtropical and exotic tropical fruits also appreciate natural gardening techniques. Citrus fruits love compost, avocados kind of make their own mulch but love to be fed with natural fertilizers, and bananas thrive in soils enriched by copious amounts of organic matter. They are no different from deciduous trees in that they appreciate a healthy soil that is rich in all of their favorite nutrients. Fruiting plants of this kind actually respond so well to natural gardening practices that many commercial growers have given up their toxic chemicals in favor of growing their crops the way nature intended. We should discuss a few of the more popular subtropical and exotic tropical fruit varieties and their specific needs so that those of you who live where they can be grown can take advantage of their delicious abundance.

Avocados

Avocados are considered evergreen trees but do have the tendency to drop all of their leaves right before growing a flush of new ones. This discarding of leaves is the reason avocados always have a thick layer of their own mulch. This prevents competing plants from taking hold where avocados are growing, and also increases the quality of the soil under the tree. Some avocado trees can reach heights over 50 feet, but popular, modern varieties normally stay around 25 to 30 feet tall. When an avocado is in bloom, it literally covers itself with thousands of tiny greenish-yellow flowers. Unfortunately, only a small percentage of them are actually pollinated and become fruit. Avocados are self-fruitful, but they like a few friends around of the same hybrid for better yields. They don't tolerate temperatures below 32 degrees Fahrenheit, and will die in severely cold weather.

Here in Southern California, when a heavy frost sets in every few years for a couple of hours, you can see the frost line where temperatures were low enough to damage the trees. It is like someone took a flame-thrower to the trees directly below a perfectly level line, and all the trees above the line are lush and green. Avocados need to be in a sunny location in the garden and won't bloom or fruit very well if they are shaded in any way. Pruning of avocados is pretty simple. Cut out dead or dying wood, and keep them shaped within the space you have for them. Avocados are heavy feeders and require a steady source of nutrients. This is one of the reasons they respond so well to natural care.

Bananas

Banana trees look more like tropical houseplants than the fruit trees we are used to. They have very soft stems and produce paddle-shaped large leaves that get torn in the wind. In parts of Florida, California, and southern Texas, bananas can be grown successfully; and huge yields of fruit can be enjoyed from them.

Bananas grow like very large grasses. They form clumps and can get all over the place if not controlled. Bananas bloom from the center of their growth, and when the crop is ripe, that particular piece of the plant dies. There are several types of bananas that can be grown by home gardeners with the right climate or a tall greenhouse other than the ones we are used to seeing in the supermarket. My favorite one is called the "Ice Cream" banana, but there are beautiful dwarf trees that produce the Cavendish, and taller trees that produce the plantain of Cuban cuisine. The Red Manzano banana is an unusual variety that can be grown in the home garden. And then there is the Ladyfinger, whose delicate flavor is heavenly.

Bananas don't like the cold! Don't even think about growing them outside if temperatures in your area commonly go below freezing. Bananas love to grow in soil enriched by compost and mulch and prefer a very sunny and warm location in the garden. They are very heavy feeders because they grow so fast. Pruning bananas is basically done to keep them in a certain area of the garden by root pruning, or to remove the spent growth of the previous crop. Bananas really don't take any special skills to grow successfully; they just have very specific climatic requirements. There are a few successful banana orchards in the United States that grow mostly the gourmet varieties. A banana orchard is an interesting place to visit. It kind of smells like bananas.

Citrus Fruits

Citrus trees are some of the most extraordinary plants in the world. The untrained observer would never know if she or he was looking at an orange, tangerine, lemon, lime, citron, grapefruit, mandarin, or just a plain old tangelo. Citrus trees are easy to grow and require little specialized care in the right conditions. They enjoy lots of sun and prefer a warm location in the garden. Since dwarf trees have come into popularity, you don't need a lot of room to grow a bunch of fruit. Citrus trees are very prolific producers of fruit, and a single dwarf tree can produce more oranges than a family of four can possibly eat. Just imagine what a 20-foot-tall standard tree can produce. When citrus trees go into blossom, the fragrance is intoxicating. I have driven or walked through orange groves in full bloom and been overcome by the smell. When we were kids, we would always know when the heat of summer was about here, as the smell of citrus blossoms was in the air, everywhere.

Citrus fruits are kind of neat for people who can grow them because they mostly ripen in the wintertime. This gives you the benefit of fresh winter fruit when your deciduous trees are dormant. Citrus trees love compost, they just can't get enough of the stuff. Whenever I'm asked by someone having trouble growing citrus what to do, I tell him or her to mulch around the tree with some compost, and then keep putting mulch around the tree each year. It works!

Citrus trees seem to respond more quickly than other plants to the mineral abundance in compost. I have seen trees with severe zinc and iron chlorosis recover in a single summer when compost and mulch are applied to the soil around them. Citrus trees don't really require much special feeding—other than to provide them with a lot of it. They are very heavy feeders and will respond to the abundant food by producing even more fruit. Pruning of citrus trees is normally only done to remove dead wood and to try and keep the inside of the tree clear of growth. Other than that, they are just shaped.

There is a person who lives in my town who has an eight-foot tall hedge of mandarin oranges lining his driveway. Citrus trees can be shaped into squares, globes, or whatever you like. I haven't seen any good topiary citrus trees, but then I haven't been looking for any. I can't wait for someone to send me a picture of a lime tree shaped like a rhinoceros. Citrus trees can tolerate temperatures in the 20s and even in the teens, but they don't really like it very much. And if there is fruit on them when the temperatures gets that low, "Fuggedaboudit." No citrus fruit can take temperatures that low and survive without some tissue damage. And citrus fruit that has been severely damaged by frosts usually ends up as frozen concentrated orange juice instead of being sold at the fresh produce market. Citrus trees prefer warm temperatures and will enjoy it if you plant them in warm climates.

Figs

Figs are actually evergreen fruit trees grown in climates where they lose their leaves during cooler winter temperatures. Figs are incredible prolific trees that can get as tall as 40 feet in some areas. Figs prefer a warm and sunny location in the garden but can actually handle a little bit of shade in hot summer areas. They need little pruning and should only be cut for the removal of dead wood and for shaping. Fig trees bleed a latex sap that gets everywhere when they are pruned, so wear old clothes when working on your fig trees. They like moist soil conditions and really appreciate a thick mulch layer over their roots.

There are several varieties and colors of fig fruit. They are very tasty right off of the tree and have their place in the kitchen for exotic desserts and ethnic cuisine as well. Figs produce lots of fruit, and birds really like them, too, so be prepared to share some with the local wildlife if you don't take steps to keep them away. One of the easiest ways to have trouble with the health of your fig threes is to allow fallen fruit to rot on the ground underneath them. Take fallen fruit to the compost pile, and give your worms a treat. It is a good thing to remember that fig trees can get quite large in width as well as height, so plant carefully when you pick a spot for a fig tree. The delicious fruit the tree yields is definitely worth the loss of garden space. Their foliage is also very attractive and can be a striking backdrop for ornamental plantings.

Guavas

Most guavas are also evergreen trees that lose their leaves because winter temperatures are not quite warm enough for them to remain on the tree. There are two evergreen plants that are called guavas. The feijoa or pineapple guava is a common shrub in areas with mild climates. The seedy blue-green fruit of this plant is very tasty and sweet. The feijoa can be planted as an ornamental shrub with a flavorful bonus. It has lovely flowers and produces fruit profusely.

Another shrub whose fruit is commonly called a guava is the psidium or strawberry guava, which produces a multitude of small, seedy red fruit. It tastes pretty good, but the shrub itself is very beautiful. Most guavas are tropical trees that produce extremely sweet and flavorful fruit. They are much like the fig when it comes to care, but they're smaller trees. Most guava trees will not take temperatures below freezing. Pruning a guava tree is done for shape and to remove dead wood only. Some of the Mexican varieties have pinkish fruit that is just out-of-this-world good to eat. Guava trees are also heavy feeders and appreciate a thick layer of mulch over their roots. Like figs, the best way to keep guavas free from diseases and pest infestations is to keep fallen fruit from rotting on the ground. Once you taste your first fruit, though, I somewhat doubt that you'll be letting too many of these gems hit the ground.

Mangoes

Mangoes are a tropical treat that can be enjoyed by gardeners in the warmest of climates here in the United States. (There are a few mango groves in my neighborhood, and I frequently trade gardening advice for fruit.) There are very specific temperature requirements for growing mangoes. Temperatures cannot fall below 45 or 50 degrees Fahrenheit or they won't survive. Pruning is only done to remove dead wood and to keep the center of the tree clear. Mangoes won't get very tall (maximum 15 feet) outside of their tropical homeland. They will, however, produce a lot of fruit if conditions are right. They need a sunny and very warm spot in the garden.

Papayas

Papayas are easier to grow and are a little more tolerant of cooler temperatures than mangoes. Papayas have beautiful foliage and can make an interesting addition to the ornamental garden—especially when four-pound fruit are hanging off of the trunk. Papayas don't require pruning, but they do appreciate a sunny spot that is protected from the wind and cold. They can get up to about ten feet tall in a few years and begin fruiting soon after they reach about four feet in height. Papayas really love compost and mulching. They are heavy feeders and appreciate the reliable supply of nutrients provided by natural fertilizers and plant foods.

We didn't go into too much detail on tropical and subtropical fruits because it would sound like I was trying to rub my climate in your face. Truth be known, I would give you mangoes and papayas for cherries. And I'll trade my guavas for your pears any day. Let's talk about feeding your fruit trees.

Feeding and Timing of Fruit Tree Fertilization

Most subtropical and tropical fruit trees are not overly particular with respect to when they are fed. Deciduous fruit trees will drop an entire crop right off the tree if they are fed at the wrong time, however. Timing when to feed your trees should be done with a little care and understanding of when the tree actually wants to be fed. It is good to remember that with our mulch layer and composts, we are really feeding our trees constantly. That is why some of the heavy-feeding tropical plants and subtropicals love their compost and mulch so much. While these materials decompose and improve the soil, they also provide nutrients to the plants in small quantities. So it is safe to say that if you have a mulch layer under your trees, you have a constant food supply available to them. This is one of the advantages of natural gardening. We feed the soil and let the soil feed the plant.

The key to feeding your trees with natural fertilizers is to time it so that the maximum amount of nutrition is available to your trees when they need it most. *When do my trees need food the most?* you might ask. Well, here's the answer. *Deciduous trees actually do most of their growing while the fruit is ripening on the tree.* But that is definitely not when you want to feed them. I feed my deciduous fruit trees in the late fall after all the leaves have fallen, and right after I harvest the last fruit from the tree. With apples and pears, that may end up being about the same time. I try to feed deciduous fruit trees and evergreen subtropicals twice a year and no more. During the late fall feeding, I make sure to supplement the minerals that I know my trees will need in the following year. This is normally some phosphorus, a little sulfur, some zinc, and a truckload of calcium.

My deciduous trees get whatever copper they will be needing from the dormant spray of Bordeaux I do a little later in the dormant period, and the fossilized kelp (Kelzyme) I use to supplement calcium. I also put down a very slow-release source of nitrogen that won't even begin to be available to the plant for six weeks. And with the cold temperatures, by then the tree is not likely to come out of dormancy anyway. The cold soil temperatures also keep the nitrogen from converting too fast into available plant food. This is where I use feather meal or hoof and horn meal. These nitrogen sources take a very long time to begin being available to the plant. When spring hits and the soil warms, this material is fully integrated into the soil and begins to release its nutrients to the fruit tree in subtle amounts. By the time the tree has fully leafed out and young fruit are hanging from it, there is an abundance of available nutrients ready for the tree to use as it sees fit. Then when the last fruit is harvested, I give it a boost of fast-acting nitrogen such as bat guano or blood meal.

This second fertilization actually helps the plant to store energy for the dormant period and assures me that when spring comes, it is ready to roll. I never feed the trees late in the season, and since most of my fruit is gone by the middle of July, I have no fear that the added nutrients in my second feeding will cause my trees to put on too much new growth that won't have time to harden before the winter chill sets in. For those of you in areas where very early frost is common, I suggest a single feeding for your trees timed close to when the last leaves fall from the tree. And no fast-acting fertilizers! Just give your tree the slow-release stuff such as feather meal or hoof and horn meal, along with whatever minerals your soils require to reset the balance of nutrients. I often say that it is better to wait for fertilizer to work than watch it work and wonder if your plant will survive the growth flush. Subtle foods are better.

When it comes to subtropical and tropical fruit, I try to time my feeding a month before the trees normally go into bloom and right after I harvest. If my citrus blooms in July, I feed them once in June with a high-nitrogen mix that has phosphorus and potassium in it, along with a few other trace minerals. If my harvest is in November,

I feed them with a mineral mix and some slow-release nitrogen in December. So I feed most of my evergreen and tropical fruit every six months. Once in the winter and once in the early summer or late spring is what I have found to be the best feeding schedule for me.

Let's take a look at some of the recipes I use for feeding fruit trees. You can adjust them to fit your special needs. Once again, if you are not inclined to mix your own plant foods, use the ones that are out on the market. Just try to make sure that they do not contain a whole bunch of fast-acting nitrogen. It can really mess things up.

<u>Fall minerals for deciduous fruit trees</u>

5 parts hoof and horn meal or feather meal
5 parts fossilized kelp (Kelzyme), lime, or gypsum
   (remember your pH)
2 parts soft rock phosphate
1 part New Jersey greensand

I apply this at the dripline of the tree at a rate of 2 cups for every inch of trunk diameter. For instance, if the tree had a trunk diameter of 6 inches, I would apply 12 cups of this material to the tree at the dripline. I measure trunk diameter about a foot up the trunk. A good time to add another layer of mulch for next season is after application of this fertilization. Then, the mulch has the entire winter to insulate the soil while it begins to decompose.

<u>Post-harvest fertilizer for deciduous fruit trees</u>

1 part bat guano
1 part kelp meal

I apply this material at a rate of one cup per every inch of trunk diameter. Don't forget to water. This is a fast-acting material and should not be used if there is a danger of early frost in your area. If your fruit is off of the tree by early July, there is no danger. If not, wait until fall, and use the slow-release mix above as a guide.

Post-harvest food for subtropical and tropical fruit trees

4 parts hoof and horn meal or feather meal
2 parts shrimp meal
5 parts fossilized kelp (Kelzyme), lime, or
    gypsum (remember your pH)
2 parts soft rock phosphate
1 part Sul-Po-Mag

I use this mixture at a rate of 3 cups per inch of trunk diameter at the dripline, water it thoroughly, then cover it with a layer of mulch. Then I water the mulch.

Pre-bloom or early summer food for subtropical and tropical fruit

5 parts alfalfa meal
2 parts fish meal
3 parts shrimp meal
1 part Sul-Po-Mag
1 part bone meal

Apply this mixture at a rate of 2 cups per inch of trunk diameter at the dripline of the tree, and water thoroughly after application.

These products are easy to find, and if stores in your area don't carry them, they can be purchased online or by mail from some of the vendors in the Resources section of this book.

Your fruit trees will love you for tending to their needs with natural gardening practices and natural materials. The reward you will receive is tons of delicious fruit and the peace of mind in knowing that the peach you just ate is . . . 100% peach. No chemicals—just the way nature intended.

Chapter Seven

ORNAMENTALS, NATURALLY

In most parts of the country, the residential garden is primarily an ornamental landscape garden. The residential landscape in this country receives more than ten times the insecticides, fungicides, herbicides, and plant foods that an equivalent size farm would ever use. Some of the chemicals that home gardeners can buy right off of the shelves are actually restricted materials for farmers due to their toxicity. A farmer desiring to use Dursban (a common ant killer and general insecticide) has to sign a bunch of papers and have a permit to use this stuff, as well as a certificate of training on how to use it.

A home gardener, frustrated by his or her ant problem, can walk right in to a local garden or home center and buy the same material without any knowledge of how harmful the material is other than the warnings on the label. I have experimented with customers of a very nice local nursery in my area to see what they remember about the bottle of chemical pesticide they have in their hands. My experiment showed that patrons of the nursery remembered vividly which pests the bottle said the material would eradicate, but had no idea of any of the warnings or the rate of application suggested on the container. This is a frightening thing. Our propensity to "nuke the bastards" has led us to purchase highly toxic materials and haphazardly apply them to our own personal spaces. We'll never hear any objections to this behavior from the chemical manufacturers. They like it when we find out that Malathion doesn't affect our aphids any longer and we have to start using Diazinon. Then we're stuck with a bottle of Malathion three-quarters full in our garages or gardening sheds until the end of time.

This cycle of poison use is becoming quite the epidemic as insects develop a resistance to so many of the chemical materials, forcing us to use more toxic chemicals to do a job that a sharp jet of water would do very effectively. In this section of the book, we will discuss some alternatives to chemical use in the home landscape, and with this information, I hope that you will be able to see that what's bugging your geraniums probably will not require a carpet bombing attack of dangerous chemicals.

The natural landscape is a place alive with checks and balances. One day you may notice a bunch of pests on one of your prized plants, and two days later all that's left are their carcasses. This is because you have allowed Mother Nature to do her work. The natural way may be a little slower, but the pests in your garden are food for something else. The trick is to help bring the predator to the prey, and nature takes care of that very effectively with airborne scents and pheromones that we can neither smell nor detect in any way. This is the unseen part of the natural garden that is just teeming with activity. It's kind of a good guy versus bad guy dynamic that goes on tirelessly. The hardest part for me, or any other gardener for that matter, is to have the patience for it to work.

Nature is a very efficient controller of outbreaks. If there is an outbreak of aphids on your prized Shasta daisies, nature brings predatory animals and insects to those perennials as a result of chemical signals put out by the plants and aphids. Predators sense a food supply and hone in on the signal. When they find the outbreak on your daisies, it's dinnertime. The most satisfying part of this process is that no synthetic materials had to be used to make it happen. Another good thing is that the aphids cannot develop a resistance to this kind of pest control. They are being eaten, and although it sounds brutal, it is by far the most effective way to keep a species population in check. No matter where you live, some insect pests and disease organisms exist. But the neat thing is that no matter where these pests and diseases live, predatory and other antagonistic life forms live as well. So the moral is, if we don't interrupt or interfere with nature, she finds a way. It just takes some time, and, most important, some patience on our part.

Flowers and Shrubs in the Natural Garden

When we bring plants into our ornamental gardens, it is because we like them as they are, or that we can envision how they will look in time. Although I love green landscapes, I am particularly drawn to colorful displays of flowering shrubs mixed with greenery. It adds flavor and some interest to the garden, not to mention a direct expression of the gardener's creativity. Caring for green and flowering plants to ensure they continue to put on a show of their beauty is a challenge to any gardener. A display of well-tended plants around your home is a way to say to admirers that you care about your surroundings and that these plants have a good home. And this is something that they can appreciate, especially if they are your neighbors. Taking the next step in understanding how these ornamental gardens can be richer is the playground of the natural gardener.

I love to see a landscape where there is a layer of mulch placed under all of the shrubs in an orderly manner. That says to me that the gardener really cares about his or her roses and camellias, because that gardener is making sure that the soil these plants are growing in is being cared for so the plants will live a long and productive life. How many people do you see in your neighborhood who are constantly replacing plants they installed only a few weeks or months before? They dig and dig and make no connection between the quality of the soil and the health of their plantings.

You may hear things such as, "I just can't get these blasted gardenias to grow in my soil," or "These darned azaleas just keep dying." They will even say that the soil conditions are to blame but won't make the connection. To gardeners like these, the soil is merely a place where the plants anchor their roots and has little or no part in the overall vigor of their garden. They will spend hundreds or thousands of dollars to keep their gardens looking like they just came off of the pages of Hearst's *Country Living* magazine, but they don't understand how or why they have failure after failure.

If we were to think of plants in our landscapes like they were animals in a reputable zoo, wouldn't we make sure that the penguin enclosure was cold, or that the tropical birdcages were warm? Plants are no different. If you want to grow gardenias and azaleas, give them what they need, and begin with the soil. A living soil will provide your landscape-planting investment with all of the things any plant requires. It is up to you to manipulate the soil to accommodate special requirements, but the main thing is to keep that soil alive. In the Old Testament of the Bible, there is a chapter where a litany of "begats" and "begots" refer to the lineage of the human race. Well, the nitty-gritty of this rather long roster of names is that without life, there is no more life. Or life begets life. This is a statement that could not be truer when talking about soils. A living soil begets more life, and that life force ends up as a healthy landscape full of flowering plants and bright green shrubs.

Choosing Shrubs and Flowers

When choosing landscape shrubs and flowers, there are a few things to consider. Is the plant you like capable of thriving in your climate, and does it have special watering requirements that would make it incompatible with the other plants where you want to put it? Does it have to be in the full sun, or will it take some shade? Does it have to be in the shade, or will it take some sun? And most of all, does it have special soil requirements?

It's difficult to get rhododendrons to thrive in a cactus garden. And it's very difficult to get cacti to thrive in a rhododendron garden. Incompatibility of plant types is one of the easiest ways to fail in the ornamental garden, or in any garden for that matter. Choosing plant types that are compatible with one another is a great way to have a successful landscape. If you love hostas and know they require some shade, why would you plant them in the full sun? Exposure to sunlight is another way to ensure that plants succeed or fail. Planting shrubs and flowers that require long exposure to direct sunlight in the deep shade of a tree or on the shady side of the house seems a little silly just to get yellow flowers for a few weeks. There are oodles of yellow flowering plants that grow well in the shade; you just need to find them. In the case of shade plants being subjected to direct sunlight, unless you are doing experiments on sunburned foliage, there is no point in trying it.

Ask your nursery professional what kind of exposure a particular plant that has caught your eye requires—they will be happy to tell you. And if you're looking for those yellow flowers that grow in the shade, ask the nursery professional if they know of any. The other thing to do when you're at the nursery or garden center looking for new plants is to look up. If you see the sun, chances are that the plants you're looking at prefer a sunny spot in the garden. If you look up and see shade fabric or it is a shady spot in the nursery, chances are that the plant prefers a spot where there is little or no direct sunlight. This is a simple observation that will save you headaches and money.

Growing shrubs and flowering plants in the garden is easy if you pay attention to a few small details. But remembering that they have to grow in the soil, and concentrating on organic matter applications in the form of composts and mulches will serve you and your plants well for years to come. Feeding your landscape shrubs and flowering plants is an easy task that only requires two applications of food per year in most climates. Remember that composts and mulches are plant foods as well, so your fertilizer and mineral supplements should focus on correcting imbalances in your soil while providing nutrients to the plants.

Most compatible arrangements of flowering and green plants in a landscape can be fed without resorting to specialized materials. There are numerous natural and organic products for general-purpose feeding of landscape plants on store shelves these days. I still prefer a simple approach to feeding the landscape. Composted chicken manure, alfalfa meal, cottonseed meal, and fish meal are all very good general-use materials that can feed your landscape very well while improving the quality of your soil—twice a year at the application rates discussed in Chapter 2 will be more than adequate. Just space the timing of your feedings so that you get the maximum effect for the length of the growing season in your area. If your growing season is six months long, feed in the early spring, and then again in three months. Some minerals to correct any imbalances are also good to add once a year or every other year. This goes back to soil testing. Have your soil tested every other year (or every year if you are so inclined) to see how your minerals are holding up. If your soil tests consistently come back stating that all is well except that you need to add calcium, just start adding more calcium, and have your soil tested every third or fourth year. I realize that staying in one place for four years goes against our upwardly mobile society, but some people do actually live in the same home for a while. Each year, add a new layer of organic mulch after you add your minerals, and leave the rest of the work to nature.

Perennials and Annuals

When we discuss perennial and annual plants in the context of the ornamental garden, we are normally discussing flowers. Flowering plants that live their entire lives in a single growing season are known as *annuals*. Flowering plants that live for more than two years and continue to return from energy stored in their roots each spring are normally referred to as *perennials*. These plants grow very quickly and use nutrients at accelerated levels, compared to most ornamental shrubs and flowering shrubs. The addition of perennial borders and annual flower beds to our gardens is one of the ways we celebrate the growing season. We plant kaleidoscopes of color to cheer up our properties and make our landscapes more interesting.

When preparing a garden space for perennials or annuals, I like to proceed as if I were planting a vegetable garden with a colorful twist. Instead of harvesting food for the tummy, I'll be harvesting eye candy. Cutting fresh flowers for the table or for decorating any room of the house with color and fragrance is a ton of fun. And the more flowers you cut, the more you get. Cutting flowers stimulates the plants to grow more of them, because their flower production is directly related to their genetic propensity to perpetuate their species.

Some flowering plants produce so much color that you must

remove flowers from them as they fade. This is called *deadheading*, and it would be a real pain if where you were working wasn't so beautiful. If you allow too many spent flowers to remain on a plant, it will stop blooming and concentrate energies on seed production. Unless you're collecting seeds, this cessation of flowering is not desirable. So trim off those flowers, and give fresh ones to your friends, although I have yet to meet any gardeners who say they have too many flowers in their garden. The spent materials make great compost, so you'll be recycling those flowers right back into the flower bed next season.

When preparing a flower bed for perennials or annuals, it is good to remember that flowering plants have greater requirements for certain minerals. In Chapter 2, we spoke of the importance of phosphorus and potassium to healthy flowering. These needs should be kept in mind. I feed a flower bed of annuals the same way I feed a veggie garden—while I'm preparing the soil. I then level it and add a mulch layer, then plant my annuals. It's quick and easy, and I don't have to worry about applying fertilizers again until I replace the spent plants with new ones and take the spent ones to the compost heap. I use a mixture of long-lasting, fast-acting natural fertilizers to ensure that my annuals receive a steady and reliable supply of what they need. Here is a sample flowerbed food for annuals.

Annual flowerbed food

2 parts feather meal
2 parts shrimp meal
1 part bat guano or seabird guano
3 parts soft rock phosphate or 4 parts bone meal
2 parts fossilized kelp (Kelzyme), lime, or gypsum
    (remember your pH)
1 part Sul-Po-Mag

This combination of nutrients produces steady growth of the plant as it develops, and profuse flowering once the plant reaches maturity. I apply this blend at a rate of 10 to 12 cups per 100 square feet of flower bed. I get sturdy plants and a healthy soil and do not have to provide supplemental fertilization, so once it is planted, I'm done (except to enjoy the "flowers" of my labors).

When caring for perennial plants, I treat them more like fruit trees. They have a distinct dormant period, so I concentrate on supplementing minerals at that time, as I do with deciduous fruit varieties. I also put down my mulch layer right before cold weather sets in, so the soil and the roots are insulated from colder weather. I give them a haircut in the fall right after they're finished for the season just as if I were pruning a fruit tree in the late winter or very early spring. This is also the time when I apply a nitrogen source to the ground that is very slow to release, such as hoof and horn meal or feather meal. This ensures that the plants have ample nutrients available when the soil warms up and they're ready to grow. When perennials are actively growing during the warm season, I feed them with a mixture of nutrient-rich materials that are fast-acting, and I repeat feedings about every two months during the growing season. These plants feed heavily, and I try not to allow them to get too hungry. My growing season mix for perennials is as follows.

Perennial flower power

2 parts cottonseed meal
3 parts alfalfa meal
2 parts shrimp meal
2 parts bone meal
1 part Sul-Po-Mag

This mixture really keeps them on their toes, and I apply it at a rate of 8 to 10 cups per 100 square feet of perennial garden space. I repeat application about every two months.

Flowers are a way to brighten up gardens without much work. I love seeing the happy faces of marigolds or pansies, and the amazing bouquets of cut flowers produced by perennials. It's fun to just sit next to a flower bed and admire the beauty of nature close up.

Roses

We could devote a whole book to roses. And, in fact, my next book is going to be called *Roses A–Z*. So in light of that, let's talk about some of the definitions of rose types, a little pruning chat, some discussion on pest control, and care techniques. Roses are far and away my favorite flowers. I like most of them, but roses just knock my socks off when I see a well-tended garden full of them. I don't really know if any other plant combines so much beauty, color, and fragrance all in one package. There are several types of roses commonly sold today. Most of them are covered by a class designation. A certain class of roses can be the *Hybrid Teas,* the *Hybrid Perpetuals, Floribundas,* and many others. Classification of roses in this manner is done as much for identification of parentage as for any other reason. Let's look at a few of the more common classes of roses and how they are cared for. But first let's get a look at some vocabulary terms that describe caring for these beauties. Let's start with *pruning*.

Definitions of Rose Pruning Techniques

<u>Hard Pruning or Low Pruning</u>

Canes are cut back to three or four buds from the base or bud union. This leaves short, sturdy canes of about 4 to 5 inches long.

Hard pruning is recommended for newly planted bush roses of the Hybrid Tea, Grandiflora, and Floribunda tribes. Hard pruning is often used by growers to produce show blooms for exhibition roses, because it produces extremely long stems. This method is not good for established garden roses and should not be practiced. It can still be used to rejuvenate sickly plants and neglected ones, but hard pruning is no longer accepted as correct pruning.

Moderate or Medium Pruning

Canes are cut back to about half of their length. Weaker stems are cut back more depending on their location on the bush.

Moderate pruning is the accepted method for treatment of established garden roses. Floribundas, Hybrid Teas, Grandifloras, and tree roses all respond best to this pruning practice. If the roses are fed well, you can expect show-quality roses on beautifully shaped bushes.

Light or High/Long Pruning

Canes are cut back to about two-thirds of their length. This means that after removal of unwanted wood, the remaining stems are merely tipped.

Light pruning is not generally recommended, as it will produce spindly bushes, and if practiced year after year, will result in an early-blooming bush with poor-quality flowers. In special cases, such as very vigorous Hybrid Teas, climbers, and shrub roses, light pruning is the only recommended way to cut these plants.

Every rose gardener employs these pruning techniques in some way or another to ensure beautiful flowers and healthy plants. We will now discuss some of the more popular classes of roses, how they are pruned when first planted, and when they are established in the rose garden. Timing of when you prune your roses is directly related to your climate. It is a good thing to consult your local nursery professional to find out when the best time to prune your roses is.

Pruning Various Types of Roses

Hybrid Tea Roses (newly planted)

Hard pruning is required to build up a strong root system and stimulate the growth of sturdy, fresh canes close to the base of the bush.

Established Roses (12 months or older)

Moderate pruning is the best method for general garden display. For show blooms, hard pruning is sometimes used. For very vigorous varieties, light pruning is recommended.

Floribunda Roses (newly planted)

Whereas Hybrid Teas should be hard pruned to a height of between 4 to 6 inches, Floribundas prefer a cane length of 6 inches

Established Roses (12 months or older)

Moderate pruning is the best way to prune Floribundas, but some old stems are hard pruned to within a few inches of the ground, while new canes that arise from the area of the base last year are only lightly pruned. This method of varying stem height will ensure a long period of continual bloom

Standard or Tree Roses (newly planted)

Hard pruning is recommended but should be less drastic than pruning for new bush roses. Stem/cane length should be about 8 inches long.

Established Roses (12 months or older)

Moderate pruning is best to form a properly balanced head, which will produce plenty of flowers. Hard pruning should be avoided on tree roses because the vigorous canes will affect the shape of the plant and make it less attractive.

Miniature and Shrub Roses (newly planted)

No pruning is required other than the elimination of any dead or broken canes that may have occurred in transit.

Established Roses (12 months or older)

Very little pruning is necessary, except for eliminating dead and sickly growth. Use scissors on miniatures instead of your pruning shears.

Climbing Roses (newly planted)

No pruning is necessary except for the removal of dead canes and tips.

Established Roses (12 months or older)

Little pruning is required apart from the removal of dead and distressed wood. Withered shoot tips with spent bloom on them should also be removed.

These rose classes are the most popular, but I do recommend that you thoroughly explore Antique roses and some of the newer hybrids from David Austin, an English rose breeder. Many of his plants are now garden favorites. He has blended some of the charm and fragrance of the old roses with some of the disease-resistant characteristics of modern roses. They are spectacular. Pest and disease control is always a chore for rose gardeners. I have included some information on disease-control techniques, as well as some pest eradication materials in this next section. Remember that mineral balances in the soil where your roses are growing, and abundant organic matter, are the first lines of defense for the natural gardener.

Pest and Disease Controls for Roses

It is widely known that roses can be a real pain in the neck if they're not attended to. This isn't the case when it comes to a rose that is allowed to grow under natural conditions, without being blasted by nitrogen-fortified chemical fertilizers and harmful insecticides and fungicides. The truth of the matter is that roses can be very easy to tend to if they are cared for with a light hand during the growing season. The fewer things that a gardener does to upset the natural balance of things, the fewer problems there will be.

Chemical insecticides are only effective until the target pest develops a resistance to that chemical. Then it becomes necessary to alternate harmful substances to control an insect population that continually gets worse because of lack of competition and lack of natural predators. The major rose pests that we encounter in the rose garden can be controlled by establishing populations of two beneficial insects, and periodic treatments with a bacterium and a tree sap extract. The two beneficial insects are the *green lacewing* and the *trichogramma wasp.*

These two insects will guard your roses against everything from aphids to some scales and spider mites. Lacewings are very active and voracious feeders whose hosts, or target prey, include aphids, mealybugs, whiteflies of some species, juvenile scale insects, and some spider mites. The tiny trichogramma wasp is a parasite of caterpillars and some species of budworms; they will also antagonize a number of other butterfly and moth species. These parasites do not have a stinger (no need to fear them); they have an ovipositor that lays her eggs inside the host. As the wasp larvae develop, they use the host as a food supply.

The bacterium that I spoke of is Bacillus thuringiensis Kurstaki, or Berliner. This product is often referred to as BT and is a paralyzing bacterium that affects many species of worms and caterpillars. By paralyzing the stomach of its host, this bacteria is very useful against its target pests.

The tree sap that I was referring to is Oil of the Neem Tree of India. The active substance in this sap has been named *azidirachtin,* after the botanical name of the tree. The extracted oils from the tissue, seeds, and sap of this tree are very effective at repelling and keeping your rose bushes free of any sign of insects. Although it smells like hazelnut, to us it has the best repellent effect on pest insects. Neem oil is sold under the name Bio-Neem, under the Safer label; and Rose Defense, under the Green Light label. These two products can be found at any garden supply store.

Controlling diseases in your rose garden is really not very difficult at all. There is no need for harmful fungicides that can cause severe physical problems or have a negative effect on outdoor pets and bees, as well as wipe out entire earthworm populations from a single spraying. Balanced nutrition and a couple of minerals can keep your garden disease free, without weekly exposure to chemicals.

Most diseases of plants will leave a healthy plant alone. It is the same with us; if we're healthy, we don't get sick. Plants also have immune systems. This is where a balanced diet that contains the proper amount of copper, sulfur, potassium, magnesium and calcium will ensure that certain very commonplace and damaging fungi don't get a foothold in your rose garden.

Potassium is very important for resistance against powdery mildew and rust on roses—not in some crazy amount that is available to the plant in five seconds after application, but instead, long-lasting natural sources from mineral deposits or from other natural sources. When potassium is broken down in the soil, it will actually help to prevent the onset and spreading of powdery mildew and rust, which are tough problems for most chemical gardeners to control. High calcium levels along with an abundance of naturally available magnesium will cause your roses to produce thick, healthy canes without the problem of slow root development in heavy soils. Copper and sulfur are the two elements I use as a spray fungicide if absolutely necessary. Other than dormant spraying, minimal spraying should be necessary to prevent fungi and disease if the roses are fed naturally.

Rose Feeding

Roses grow very fast, so use a lot of food to continue to produce bloom after bloom over a period of up to eight months out of the year. This has been the great sales pitch of the chemical fertilizer producers in an effort to get you out in your garden every 7 to 14 days using their products on your roses. I can't spend that much time fertilizing, and most people won't do it even if they are regular users of these chemical products.

Natural fertilizers are released after the natural biodegradation process occurs in the soil, which enriches the soil as the rose plant is fed with a balanced supplement. Natural fertilizers are also often very long-lasting, thus minimizing the release of carbon dioxide from the soil (remember those greenhouse gases?). The use of chemical fertilizers in residential as well as agricultural and industrial applications is responsible for a great deal of greenhouse gas escaping from our soils. When natural fertilizers are used, a process known as *carbon sequestration* occurs. Carbon is the universal filter, sponge, and storage facility for toxins, and assists in the creation of environments where organisms can survive with a greater degree of health. Remember that most filters that remove impurities from water are different grades of carbon. When soils digest natural fertilizers, they do so with bacteria and a number of microorganisms. Organic matter is turned to food, and plants can achieve a greater level of health in these conditions. No speed is lost, nor are roses any smaller or fewer in numbers when fed naturally. They are just healthier and more trouble free.

Natural rose foods are used less often due to their slow rate of release into the soil. This means, of course, fewer trips into the garden to feed your roses, resulting in less work and smaller cash expenditures on fertilizers. This equation certainly seems logical.

Several good organic rose foods are produced on the open market. Whitney Farms produces the most recognized natural rose food, and it is very good. The Grow More Company also produces a superior rose food that can be purchased at many garden centers. Over the years, I have developed a rose fertilizer that works very well and is used less often than all of the commercial brands. It has been broadcast on the television and radio, and it also appears regularly in a score of local newspapers and magazines across the United States and Canada in my gardening columns. The recipe is as follows:

Don's favorite rose food

1 part hoof and horn meal
1 part seabird or bat guano
1 part cottonseed meal
2 parts soft rock phosphate or bone meal
1 part fossilized kelp (Kelzyme) or kelp meal

The resulting plant food is applied to the roses at a rate of 1 to 2 cups per rose (depending on size and age), every 60 days at the dripline of the plant. During an eight-month growing period, that is only four applications to ensure proper plant nutrition. Not only will this rose food do its job, but will also improve your garden soil while it works to feed your rose bushes.

I would like to address the users of Epsom salts in the feeding of their roses. Tap water is salty, and our air is salty, and our soil is salty. Why would we want to add more sodium and more chloride to this mix intentionally? I know that it works, but after the salt builds up to toxic levels, then other problems begin to show up. I suggest the use of Sulfate of Potash Magnesia instead of Epsom salt as a magnesium source. Sul-Po-Mag is very inexpensive and goes a long way. You are also applying more that just magnesium. This mined mineral compound is rich in potassium, which we know as the third number in commercial fertilizers and its disease- and fungus-fighting capabilities. The small amount of sulfur in this product is very useful for reasons previously discussed. One cup per rose during the dormant period will do all of the things that Epsom salt does, without the salinity and the problems associated with salinity. Sul-Po-Mag breaks down more slowly, so the plant gets a regular supply of these nutrients. Epsom salts is 100% water-soluble, and what isn't immediately used by the plant is either washed from the surface of the soil during rain or is leached away by rain or irrigation. Sul-Po-Mag can be purchased at many garden centers. This product is only applied once a year.

I would like to stress the importance of a good layer of organic compost or mulch in the rose garden. This is fuel for the many organisms that make soil rich and healthy. Any commercial compost can be used, but homemade is the best. Remember that organic matter is the food of earthworms. More compost=more earthworms=more porous soil that accepts water better and doesn't dry out nearly as fast= savings on the monthly water bill.

I grow roses, I can't wait for spring to see my roses, and I am addicted to roses. Hello, my name is Don, and I am a Rosarian. I don't know if there is a 12-step program for recovering rose addicts, but I figure that an addiction to roses really can't hurt anyone—a few scratches, maybe, but I'll pick this addiction over any others. The rewards are too great for me to quit. And I've never heard of anyone getting thrown in the slammer for being bonkers about a flower. So I figure that roses are a pretty safe thing to be hooked on.

Roses are just one of the many ornamentals that can be successfully grown in containers. Container gardening of ornamental plants and flowers is something any aspiring gardener can do.

Potted Plants

Growing ornamentals in pots goes back a long way. The ancient Asian art of *bonsai* literally means "pot plant." I have seen century-old plants cared for in this way, and I find it one of the most incredible expressions of artistic talent I have ever witnessed.

Just like growing vegetables in containers, ornamentals are only limited by the creativity of the gardener. Container gardening of flowers and other ornamental plants can express the season in the case of a poinsettia or an Easter lily, or it can be a testimonial to the skill of a gardener, like in orchid growing.

I'm in it for the fun. I like to grow annual flowers mixed with lettuce, or basil mixed with red-leafed begonias. I go to a garden center with a container in my hand, or an idea of a container I would like to fill, and just go for it. The rules are few. Just pick plants with compatible watering and sunlight requirements that won't crowd one another out. That's it—from there, anything goes. I love seeing containers of flowers line a walkway up to a front entry of a home. It's like the residents are saying, "We're colorful and interesting people." They probably are, too. It seems that wherever I go and whatever I do, I always come back to gardeners. Maybe it's their passion for living things or their nurturing spirit. Whatever it is, I have yet to meet an avid natural gardener without a zest for life and a deep appreciation for how things work in nature.

The only thing that container gardening of ornamentals requires other than a cool pot and some plants is potting soil. We discussed my favorite potting soil blends back in our discussion on vegetables. I use the same mixes for ornamentals. There are some good potting soils out there that are ready to use. I can't make a decision on which one works best for you, but I do urge you to experiment with different mixes until you find one that suits your needs.

When it comes to feeding container gardens of any kind, I like to use liquid fertilizers and normally find that a combination of fish solubles (fish emulsion) and liquid kelp products works best for me to ensure that plants get everything they require in the form of nutrients. I try to feed actively growing plants about every four to six weeks, and when plants are a little slow, I like to give the a taste of compost or guano tea. That usually perks them right up. Watering is the most important thing to monitor when growing plants in containers. They have a limited soil area to draw moisture from and cannot send roots out to look for water. So keep them moist, and you'll be the beneficiary of brilliant displays of beauty that you created in partnership with nature.

It's Easy to Do

Caring for your ornamental plants by using natural gardening practices is a very simple thing to do. And once you get the hang of it, your garden will be a glorious place of natural beauty. A good thing to remember is to concentrate the bulk of your efforts on creating and maintaining a living soil that has balance minerals and a reliable supply of nitrogen. Everything else is just mulch. Your home landscape can be a place of great enjoyment, and without the fear of chemical residues and toxic pollutants in it, you will be truly creating a personal Eden. That is certainly the way nature intended it to be.

Chapter Eight

THE GREEN, GREEN GRASS OF HOME

A lush, verdant-green lawn is part of American culture. We spend hours trimming and mowing so that our green carpet is better looking than anyone else's. One commercial shows a couple of neighborhood gorillas making fun of the poor sap with the brown lawn area. He is left thinking that he is less than a man if his lawn isn't as green as Bubba's. So he goes down to the garden center and picks up $500 worth of super chemicals to make his lawn perfect. Just like the stuff Bubba uses. This all happens in 15 seconds. How can anything compete with those three garden experts sitting out on their front lawns discussing the latest nuclear lawn food? No one ever says anything about the toxic runoff from these concentrated chemicals or the fact that their children and dogs are brain damaged from playing on this chemical slick disguised as grass. They just continue chuckling about how amazing Super Green or Insta-Green worked on their lawn and how they are the envy of the neighborhood.

I wonder when Soylent Green will be a plant food for turf. We get could old Chuckie Heston out there with an M-16 or some kind of grenade launcher shooting weeds and napalming insects screaming, "Soylent Green is for lawns!" Now that would sell some chemicals for sure. I saw this Dursban (a potent insecticide) commercial while watching my local NFL team get their butts kicked, where this guy puts the Dursban into the spreader and then begins laughing insanely about the mayhem he's creating on the pest population in his lawn while he applies it. I couldn't believe that some ad agency actually got paid for thinking something like that up. And then I thought of Moses and Soylent Green, and it made perfect sense.

We natural gardeners can have a perfect lawn without all of those fancy names and without spending $5,000 a year to keep a postage stamp-sized turf area perfectly coiffed and green. We also won't be spending any money on therapy for our cretinous dog that played too much on the green chemical slick and has now taken to sniffing lawnmower exhaust fumes for fun.

The Natural Lawn

The natural lawn can really be the envy of the entire neighborhood. The techniques used to grow nutritious vegetables, succulent fruit, and stunning ornamentals easily translate to turf care. When we focus on promoting biological diversity in the soil beneath our turfgrasses instead of annihilating everything alive within a square mile, our lawns can be better, cheaper to maintain, and at least as green as Bubba's. By targeting and excluding life from the soil, chemical gardeners miss the whole Biblical twist to effective stewardship. Death and destruction of the soil ecosystem beget death of turf and a ludicrous dependency on rescue chemicals. And instead of turning the lawn area into Chernobyl or another Love Canal, a natural gardener can turn his or her lawn into a safe place for their children to play that holds its beauty because there is so much going on in the soil underneath the lawn. Life begets life.

A natural lawn grows in soil that is alive and whose roots can reach deeper, thanks to earthworms and other garden helpers. The natural lawn doesn't stress as easily in extremely hot or cold weather and doesn't need watering as often, because the soil and all of its organic matter holds on to water better. A natural lawn doesn't require feeding every week or two, and most natural lawns only require two feedings per year. A natural lawn supplies the rest of the garden with superfast compost and stays green all the while. Natural lawns don't harm the health of your children because of the high nitrogen content blocking oxygen to their brains. And while Bubba's kids are sucking the cream filling out of their Twinkies with spouts from the gas can because they forgot about straws, your children will be playing Twister on the lawn, safe from cretinism.

What to Do with the Clippings

Grass clippings are a rich source of valuable nitrogen to the lawn and to the compost pile. The new mulching mowers that have become so popular these days actually double-chop the clippings and return them to the lawn to be eaten by beneficial microorganisms or by Aristotle's plows of the Earth (earthworms). In the compost heap, those grass clippings can speed up the decomposition of other harder-to-decompose materials making your compost ready to use sooner.

If you have the room and you're willing to make your own compost, never throw grass clippings away. They are the best compost accelerators a home gardener and composter can use. But in my humble opinion, the best place for grass clippings is back on the grass. The amount of biological activity that is stimulated by returning this nitrogen-rich organic matter back into the lawn is astounding. And with the advent of the mulching lawnmower, the task is no more difficult than mowing the lawn was in the first place.

I have seen gardeners spread out their grass clippings like mulch. I like that idea as long as the clippings don't dry out and actually keep water from entering the soil by creating a crust over it. I have also spoken to gardeners who save their clippings until they prepare the soil for their vegetable garden. They just add the clippings along with the other minerals and till it right into the soil. I like this idea very much. Using grass clippings as a soil conditioner is a very good idea. They add nitrogen to the soil and they are an easily digested material for the beneficial microbes in the soil as well as the earthworms. Grass clippings can be used in many places in the natural garden and should not be disposed of, even if you are not inclined to make your own compost.

Superfast Compost

Grass clippings are one of the key ingredients in making really fast compost for use in the garden. Grass clippings can be mixed with a number of other green materials and some smaller particle brown materials to make ultrafertile compost in about seven to ten days. I can't wait to mow the lawn when I need some extra compost because I know that in a few days I'll get what I need, and then the garden will get what it needs. The trick is to mix the clippings and other materials thoroughly and then turn the compost every day.

There are several compost tumbler-type containers manufactured for this purpose. I use a trash can with a lid that closes tightly. I then cut some slots in the can all over the place so air can circulate while the lid is closed. I do not cut *holes,* because the material will escape from the container, so I cut *slots.* I fill it with grass clippings; kitchen scraps, and some smaller brown material that has been chopped. I mix it all together and roll the can around a few times, then stand it upright. I do this every day for about a week or so, opening the can each day to see if there is enough moisture in the material. In seven to ten days, I have superfast and superfertile compost for the garden. I sometimes chop the brown material by putting it in a pile and lowering the lawnmower down onto it. That normally does the trick in making the brown portion of my superfast compost small enough to be digested quickly. So I lost a trash can, but I get compost!

Chemical Lawn Fertilizer Problems

Besides the obvious reasons, chemical plant foods are dangerous for another reason as well. The high-powered nitrate nitrogen in these plant foods has the capacity to make plants grow like crazy. It also has the ability to cause some very debilitating health problems for those who come in contact with them. A health problem known as Blue Baby Syndrome is the depletion of oxygen to the brain caused by an overabundance of nitrogen in a particular environment. If high-nitrogen fertilizers are used to make your lawn as green as Bubba's, your pets and children could be affected by this.

Blue Baby Syndrome is a known problem, and it can be directly linked to nitrogen-enriched environments. This is one of the most compelling reasons why using high-nitrogen chemical lawn foods may not be a very good idea if your children like to play on your lawn. This may also be a problem for your pets if they spend a lot of time on the lawn. An oxygen deficiency to the brain can cause irreparable damage and actually make an animal affected by this phenomenon suffer from cretinism, an illness of reduced brain function. I don't use chemical lawn fertilizers, so I can use the few brain cells I own that are still functioning. Even though I'm joking a little here, I assure you that Blue Baby Syndrome is a real problem that can directly affect the health of your family.

Natural Foods for Lawns

Feeding your lawn with natural products and materials depends on creating a living system in the soil your lawn is growing in. Natural turf care and feeding count on materials such as compost to increase biological activity in soils in order to make the natural plant foods work faster and for longer periods of time to keep your lawn lush and green. Natural lawn foods average less than half the nitrogen, and many are less than a third as strong as their chemical counterparts. When I feed a lawn or counsel a gardener on feeding their lawn, I try to inform them of the many things that natural lawn foods do for the soil, and the many other significant contributions they provide for the overall vigor of the lawn ecosystem.

Turf grass is not a natural thing. It is the challenge of gardeners, and especially natural gardeners, to make this unnatural gathering of plants into an efficiently functioning system of biological processes resulting in an emerald-green lawn. This can be a daunting task when it comes to weed control, and pest and disease control, and then there's always Bubba to tell you you're a loon for not using Soylent Green on your lawn just like he does. Feeding a lawn with natural materials is pretty easy when you think of it. All you need is some finely screened compost, the minerals to balance your soil, and a subtle source of nitrogen.

The touchy subject of providing a lawn with large doses of nitrogen is not an issue when caring for the lawn naturally. The amounts of nitrogen applied to a lawn treated with natural materials is basically used to replenish lost nitrogen when clippings are not recycled back into the turf with mulching lawnmowing equipment. When clippings are recycled into the lawn mechanically, nitrogen is supplemented in small amounts to assist in the decomposition process and to provide some additional food to soil microbes so that further growth of the lawn is stimulated. Low nitrogen inputs are used to keep the engine running at peak efficiency. The key to feeding your lawn naturally is to work with the soil and then let the biology in the soil work its magic.

The materials are easy to find and are normally rather abundant. Screening your compost or buying fine-screened compost is easy to come by. Screening your homemade compost is fairly easy to do by constructing a simple screen from a wooden frame and some fine mesh chicken wire. Adding the screened material to your lawn can be done with precision compost spreaders, or you can use my method of throwing it all over the lawn in the most haphazard manner possible. I love throwing compost all over the place, because no matter where it falls on soil, it does good things. I just chuck it on the lawn and let some of it fall where it may. I guess that's one of the reasons I never have enough compost. I add compost to the lawn in the early to middle part of spring and then again in midsummer. I feed the lawn with chicken manure on the same day so that I'm not doing too much work and jeopardizing my reputation as a lazy gardener. Watering thoroughly after applying these materials gets them down where they can do the most good—in the soil. Once a year, I winterize the lawn by adding minerals only, and this is done in the fall.

Winterization

During the cool season, your lawn only requires some minerals and some organic matter to feed your soil. This lets you take a break from weekly mowings, constant feeding, and being swayed into buying the latest Bubba food that "guarantees" the best lawn in the neighborhood.

I want to tell you how to save some money, ensure better soil structure, and do a heck of a lot less work in the winter while your lawn goes through some seasonal changes. Cooler weather and cold weather create slower metabolic rates in many plants, including turf-grasses. This slower metabolism results in slower growth, less water consumption, and a drastic reduction in the need for nitrogen inputs. I actually recommend that from the first of November to the first of March, no nitrogen-rich fertilizers be applied to turfgrass in areas where winters are mild. In severe climates, this won't be a problem because no one in their right mind would feed snow.

This allows the plants to rest a little during cold weather, and minimizes potential damage to soft growth from occasional frost. Stimulating the growth of your lawn during cold weather can be dangerous, because the tender growth is susceptible to a multitude of problems—not the least of which is total tissue destruction from extreme or lingering frost. Any lawn food with a nitrogen content higher than 5% (identified as the first number of three on a fertilizer package) will unnaturally stimulate growth of your turfgrasses during cold weather. Chemical fertilizers put all or most of their nitrogen out to the plants immediately after dissolving in water. This puts way too much available nitrogen where the lawn can use it; thus, rapid growth occurs at a time of year when none should.

Lawns don't have to be growing at warp speed to remain lush and bright green. Quite the opposite is true. The chemical manufacturers want you to continue to buy their products all year, so they invent marketing strategies to convince you that your lawn really needs their products if you don't want to be the laughingstock of your neighborhood. Boy, have they got it wrong. Smart turf management professionals utilize the cool season to rebuild the mineral content in their soils and to feed the soil with a little bit of organic matter so that in the spring and summer, they don't have mineral deficiencies that can result in numerous disease and pest problems. The organic matter they add to the soil feeds beneficial microbes and larger organisms such as earthworms.

I add the organic matter earlier in the season, which helps to minimize runoff of water, increase water retention (so I don't have to water so often), and improve the physical structure of the soil. One of the best things this organic matter addition can do is stimulate the larger organisms in your soil (such as earthworms) to stay in the soil underneath your lawn, because food is there. Earthworms also have the added benefit of tunneling around in your soil, creating deeper and improved water penetration while feeding on thatch. *Thatch* is the name given to the dead and decaying remains of the summer's growth. Thatch is a good thing when a lawn is cared for naturally, because the beneficial organisms inhabiting your soil actually convert this thatch into plant food that your turf can use when the weather warms up. The whole mechanical dethatching thing that begins in the fall just cracks me up. If the people that spend all that money on removing this valuable material would just feed it to their soils they would have better soils and healthier lawns.

Winterizing your lawn should only include a mineral supplement and some organic matter, as mentioned earlier. I love to apply a good calcium source such as Kelzyme fossilized kelp or a mixture of lime or gypsum, sulfur, soft rock phosphate, and sulfate of potash magnesia (Sul-Po-Mag) at a 5-1-2-1 ratio. Apply Kelzyme or the mineral mix at a rate of 10 pounds per 1,000 square feet of turf. Water after application as always. This makes for a great winter meal for all of the good guys that live in the soil beneath your lawn.

By adding these ingredients to your lawn at this time of year, you will be truly winterizing your lawn. The other really great thing you won't be doing is contributing to the pollution problem that often occurs when chemical fertilizers run off of poorly maintained soils into the storm drain system, resulting in contamination and accelerated bacterial growth in our oceans and fresh water supplies. Just add some minerals and some organic matter, and in the spring, your lawn will be way ahead of any of the others in your neighborhood and will remain lush and green throughout the winter. And for those of you with snow on the lawn during this time of year, Bubba can't make fun of the color of the snow, can he? This mineral material can help you to grow a weed- and disease-free lawn that is resistant to pests and stays bright green all year, or until the snow covers it. Eat your heart out, Bubba.

Runoff and Soil Improvement

Lawns treated and cared for with natural materials will improve soil quality while it increases the ability of water to penetrate, and the added organic matter will allow the soil to hold water more efficiently. This improvement in the condition of the soil will result in a reduction of the chances of runoff water emanating from your lawn. This also reduces, and will eventually eliminate, runoff water from leaving your lawn as your soil conditions are gradually improved. Soon, the only rainwater that will run off of your lawn will have to come from a rather heavy downpour. When your lawn is sufficiently improved, you will not lose nutrients from your turf grass, nor will those nutrients ever end up at the beach or at the lake. Your lawn and your garden will be part of the solution to our environmental problems in this society.

Welcome to a larger world where we are part of the solution instead of part of the problem. I think nature would like it that way.

Chapter Nine

TREES—
NATURE'S GIANTS

The outright majesty of trees is something I have never been able to get over. Not that I've wanted to, believe me, but everywhere I've traveled, I've been around trees. It doesn't matter if they were palms on the beach in the Caribbean, exotic tropical hardwoods in Asia, or the giant redwoods of my home state of California—I have always been in awe of trees.

A few years back, I took a trip to northwestern Montana and stopped in to visit Glacier National Park. Now I've been to Yosemite many times, and I thought Yellowstone was amazing, but the trees at Glacier just had this incredible air of peacefulness to them. I don't know if it was because there weren't any screaming tourists, but the forest seemed very calm. There was a breeze, and the trees would "talk" a little in the wind. It was as if I had been transported to a place where no conflict could possibly exist; it had to be one of the most defining moments in my life. *We have to keep this ecosystem healthy,* I thought. I then went on my merry way, checking out the red rocks and doing other tourist stuff. I remember that moment among those hemlock trees so vividly, even today. It was as if for one single moment in time I got to really experience nature from within her system. It was an epiphany.

Planting trees in your garden may not inspire you to stand dumb-founded in their presence, but here's a little tidbit of trivia. The only life form on this planet where an individual specimen was alive at the turn of the last millennium and will still be alive at the turn of this newest one is a tree. How's that for stamina? You may not be awestruck every time you see an oak tree, nor am I. I just really think that trees are pretty interesting creatures with very long lives. There are so many varieties of trees, both evergreen and deciduous, that it would take months just to write a little something nice about a frac-tion of them. Around the home garden, trees most certainly have a place. And in the natural garden, trees can be left alone without wor-rying about things such as deep root feeders or putting tree spikes in to feed the trees. In the natural garden, the soil takes care of the trees, and you just take care of the soil once or twice a year.

Trees can provide shade that helps you save energy costs in win-ter and summer. Trees provide homes for a multitude of beneficial wildlife species. Trees can produce stunning displays of flowers and colors depending on the time of year. But my favorite thing that trees do in the home garden is holding up a hammock. I just like to lie down, looking up through the foliage, and daydream about a warm summer day, with lemonade being poured from a pitcher being held by a sundress-clad Stephanie of Monaco! Whoops, sorry about that, got a little carried away by the moment. Nevertheless, trees are pretty great garden plants that give scale and grandeur to our home gardens while keeping us cool in the summertime and providing an abundant source of oxygen to all of the humans and other animals that live near where they grow.

A Forest at Home

For those readers with large properties, I strongly suggest plant-ing a woodland habitat. It may seem like a hard thing to do, but it only takes about 15 trees and some patience. I also suggest that if you are considering planting a personal forest that you mix your trees. Plant a few flowering trees such as magnolias to lend some color and fragrance to the garden, and plant a few trees that provide color in the spring, such as pears, cherries, or crabapples. Include a few that give great fall colors or that draw birds with their fruit. And then fill the rest in with evergreens that lend their nobility and great size to the garden.

After a few years, this forest will have a canopy of protection, and you can then begin to plant the understory. Small trees such as camellias and saucer magnolias are great in the lower story of a woodland garden. Large azaleas and rhododendrons, hydrangeas, hostas, and ferns also really spruce things up. You can create a woodland garden in any part of the country with some space, a few trees, and an investment in time. The result will be a place where you can go to seek the quiet tranquility of your own woodland paradise. There are no climate restrictions here; trees grow in every part of the world where there is ample water to support their growth.

I am just nuts about New England forests habitats and have planted a few here in Southern California with similar trees that can take our heat. Once the trees got tall enough to provide shade, I got busy planting all sorts of flowering plants and forest evergreens that made each of these places seem as though they were meant to be there. And the variety of critters that these mini ecosystems supported was a sight to behold. Songbirds made homes in the trees, and a friendly hawk built a nest high in one as well. At night, owls would sit patiently waiting for a jackrabbit or mouse to start feeding in the garden so it could have dinner as well. Lizards and toads and all sorts of animals found this place, and all I had to do was some planting.

In the spring, the redbuds, hydrangeas, camellias, and azaleas bloomed, turning the place into something right out of the pages of one of Hearst's gardening magazines. People would stop and ask if they could possibly impose and walk through the stand of trees. And, of course, garden talks ensued.

During the summer, perennials would bloom, and the trees provided shade for ferns and numerous shade-loving plants. And then in the fall—bang! So much color of a different sort. When the leaves fell, the evergreens took center stage. It was a sight to behold, for sure. And all of this on just a few thousand square feet of garden space. I could go on for hours, and often do about this kind of gardening. Woodland gardens are a true natural garden because they support so much life in such a small space. And I don't feel bad for the rabbits or the mice becoming dinner for the hawks and owls because they eat the azaleas. If you ever have the chance to walk the Augusta National Golf Course in Georgia, you'll understand what I mean when I wax romantically about woodland gardens. That place will blow your mind in the springtime with its colors and textures. The grass isn't so bad, either, even if they do use synthetics. Just don't roll around on it.

The Intelligence of Shade

Growing trees in your home garden is not just a beautiful thing to do; it's a *smart* thing to do. The shade provided by these giants when they're planted near your home keeps temperatures around the house very comfortable. In the summer when people are passing out from the heat, your trees will provide a buffer for that discomfort. And when the trees are strategically planted at the south and west sides of your home, they will shade the house and help you manage the inside temperatures by keeping the house cooler. This will obviously cut down on air conditioning costs and save you some wampum, so you can take a better vacation—or send your children off to get a better education so they can support your gardening habit when you retire. The other great thing that evergreen trees do is to keep your home warmer in the winter. Trees serve as wind breaks to cut down the chilling breezes that plague residents in northern climates. They also provide measurable heat during even the coldest of times. Trees are insulators, and the shade they provide is something to look forward to when planting a tree.

Shade is also something that can be easily managed by pruning your trees to provide just as much or little shade as you desire. The amount of shade provided by different species of trees also varies. So choose your shade trees to fit your preferences, and don't be afraid to ask your nursery professional for some advice on trees with light or heavy shading capabilities. This will cut down on pruning costs and give you exactly what you're looking for.

Remember that if you want light in the winter, and you're not all that jazzed about shade when temperatures are already low, plant deciduous shade trees. They provide as much shade as you could possibly want in the summer months, a good show of color in the fall, and they allow light and air circulation during the winter when they have no leaves. This is a great benefit, and offers you even more choices as far as which trees to plant in a specific part of your garden. Don't forget about flowering shade trees; they can make a striking statement and will provide a good place to hang that hammock as well.

Leaf Litter Is Great for the Compost Pile

One thing that shade trees of all kinds do very well is dropping their leaves to the ground. This is called *leaf litter,* and it is a very valuable material for the natural gardener. These dried leaves and needles can provide you with an abundance of carbon-rich brown material for the compost heap.

The one thing that home composters seem to run out of the most is brown material to supply bulk and food to the microbes in their compost piles. This is one area where having a few shade trees planted around the yard can really help. Trees are notorious for dropping their leaves all over the place, and in the fall, they can leave a real mess. This autumn bonanza or fodder for the compost pile is a very good thing for natural gardeners, and I wish that our chemical-using counterparts would take advantage of the free mulch their trees provide. If you are not a compost producer and have a lawnmower, you can make gobs of homemade mulch for your garden from the leaves that fall off of your trees. Just rake the leaves or pine needles into a pile, and run over them a few times with the lawnmower. The machine will chop the fallen foliage, and then you can spread it around your plants as mulch. Water it very thoroughly after you've spread it over the garden, and you'll be amazed at how orderly everything looks with a nice layer of mulch around.

I never pass up an offer of fallen leaves, and since I never have enough compost, I find that the fall is a time of great anticipation. I can't wait to get new compost piles started and to use the chopped material as a mulch around fruit trees and roses. I use the really coarse stuff to replenish the pathways in the garden. Mulch is a great pathway material because it keeps weeds under control, and it looks very natural. It also keeps me from tracking mud around, and gives a home to certain beneficial insects, while it improves the quality of the soil under the path in case I decide I want to change the garden around.

But by far, the most use I get from fallen leaves is in the compost pile. I make that layer cake we discussed in Chapter 3, and eagerly anticipate the finished product, so in the spring I have almost enough compost.

I have a friend named Shannon who has been gardening naturally since we met four years ago. She and her husband, Scott, are very good people and devoted nature lovers. A year ago, Shannon bought a very large load of compost from some of my friends who produce compost commercially. When the load arrived on her driveway, she freaked and called me wondering what in the name of Pete she was going to do with all of this organic matter that was now preventing her from parking her car in the garage. I kind of chuckled, and told her where and how to spread the material in her garden. I also informed her that too much compost was an impossibility.

Two days later, after the compost had settled down and had become a part of the garden, I visited Scott and Shannon, and Shannon was already looking forward to more of the stuff. Today, Shannon is about to add another thick layer of compost to her garden, and she loves to talk about her soil. The other day after Scott and I had come back from a sailing trip, Shannon informed me that here gardenias were growing too big, and she asked how she should trim them. In this part of the country, people who are able to grow gardenias are considered gardening wizards. Shannon knows that the soil grew her precious plants, and that the soil was fortified with compost made from the leaves that fell off a bunch of trees. Understanding the cycle of life in the soil has made Shannon an extraordinary gardener with a deep appreciation of how things work. She loves her soil, and her soil transports that love to her plants.

Natural Homes for the Good Guys

Trees provide shelter for a myriad of animals. Most of them are beneficial to the garden and the gardener. Squirrels can be a problem, and that darn woodpecker just won't shut up, but for the most part, trees provide homes for the good guys.

Songbirds love to perch and nest in trees where there is food close by. And the natural garden has an abundant supply of bugs for them to eat. Raptors (hawks, owls, and eagles) love to roost in tall trees where they can get a good look at the entire garden and pick up a rabbit or a mouse snack here and there. And other beneficial critters such as toads and lizards love to creep around in the leaf litter looking for the occasional meal that may cross their path. All of these animals play an integral part in the overall complexity of a natural system. Each and every animal, all the way up to the top of the food chain, plays a part in the natural garden. The more animals, the better the system functions. Trees play a very important part in providing homes for these animals. If one were to stop and really think of how a single tree can be an entire ecosystem unto itself, we would all have a grater understanding and a greater appreciation of the role trees play in the frenetic ecology of the garden.

Ponder this: A single maple tree sits in a garden somewhere in America. In the fall, this maple tree puts on a show of spectacular color for the resident gardeners, then begins to drop its leaves. The tree is in a woodland portion of the garden, so the gardeners let the leaves lie there as they fall to the ground. Immediately, billions of microbes begin the process of turning these leaves into compost. As the microbes work in the moist, dark soil, earthworms are also grabbing chunks of partially decomposed leaves for their lunch and taking them back down into their burrows where they deposit the castings deeper in the soil fertilizing as they go. The microbes continue working below the surface, converting leaves to humus. Above the ground, millions of insects scurry around in the leaf litter, picking up their lunch on other insects and on the decaying leaf litter as well. Chasing these insects around are larger insects, which are in turn chased around by lizards, toads, and birds. Field mice eat some of the insects, and other rodents feed on them, too.

Above all of this, the predators sit at the top of the food chain. The raptors wait patiently for a lizard, mouse, or a rabbit to wander a little too far away from cover in this frantic search for food. Then they swoop. All of these animals are depositing their waste under the tree, keeping the nitrogen engine running, which feeds the microbes. That is an efficiently running system of biological miracles.

Nothing compares to the natural garden. And when the system is running well, it runs all the time—hot or cold, wet or dry. Just the way nature intended.

Chapter Ten

NATURAL
PEST CONTROL

Insects have been on this planet much longer than we have, and pre-date the dinosaurs by many millions of years. The thought of this conjures up images of dragonflies with two-foot wingspans, and three-pound cockroaches that were even bigger than New York City rats. Insects also far outnumber any other family of animals on the planet. They live in the sea, on land, and in the air. There is pretty much a bug for all occasions. The fact that they occupy every niche in the natural world makes them one of the most successful and resilient groups of critters ever to inhabit this planet.

Most gardeners rank pest control as the most challenging part of tending to a garden. The sight of a rose stem loaded with aphids or a tomato plant being consumed by gargantuan hornworms sends us running for the napalm or whatever Bubba uses. In the natural garden, these things happen as well, but instead of running for Soylent Green, we count on natural, and sometimes a few Darwinian processes to overcome the infestations. "Survival of the fittest" is a slogan often used in the natural garden. Natural gardeners promote increased vigor in our plants by feeding them with subtle foods that are processed and made available to the plants by the biological engine in the soil. Natural gardeners count on and expect periodic attacks by pest insects, but they know that the cavalry of beneficial predators will come to the rescue in short order. Instead of the rescue chemistry that our friend Bubba uses, we count on rescue biology, which is far more reliable in a garden, and harmless to our environment and us. When the first mealybug shows up and Bubba goes running for the napalm, we patiently wait for the horror movie to start.

The pre-dating of pest insects by predatory and parasitic insects and other organisms is something right out of a 1950s horror movie. Odd-looking larvae and bizarre insect adults pierce and chew their way through a pest insect infestation in the most brutal of ways imaginable. It's pure poetry to the natural gardener!

How Nature Works to Even Things Out

Ever since that first cyanobacteria we discussed earlier took its first gulp of carbon dioxide and burped its first puff of oxygen a few billion years ago, nature has been reacting to abundance and imbalances. When a particular organism or element has become too numerous or abundant, nature finds a way to check it before it becomes a threat to other balances. This can be as simple as a large increase in ladybug populations to balance out an earlier increase in aphid numbers. Or, it can be as complex as hawk and coyote population increasing in reaction to an abundant rodent population.

Natural reactions to imbalances often take the form of predation or digestion. That first cyanobacteria reacted to an environment rich in carbon dioxide by using it for respiration (inhaling it) and exhaling a different material. Fortunately for us, this material was oxygen. Anywhere on the Earth you find an abundance of a particular animal, plant, or mineral, you will find an animal, plant, or mineral that reacts to it. This reaction can be in the form of simple competition in the case of plants, or oxidation in the case of minerals. The easiest natural reaction to identify is where a reactive organism actually eats the one it is reacting to.

This cycle of eat and be eaten has continued up till today in the often-invisible world of nature. But the reactions continue. That aphid feeding on your rose bush is sending out a signal that we cannot detect. That signal may be a sign to other aphids to come and eat here, but there are other organisms that can read these signals as well. These predatory and parasitic critters get a whiff of aphid, and head off in the direction of the signal lickety-split. Soon there may be more aphids, but there are aphid midges, ladybugs, lacewings, tachnid flies, and a virtual plethora of other animals now eating and parasitizing the aphids. That pest insect never had a chance, and since the roses in your natural garden are healthy because they're living in soil that provides them with abundant nutrients, they recover quickly and are none the worse for the experience.

This kind of stuff happens every second of every day and night in a natural garden—with no holidays. And while Bubba may have eradicated his pest population before you, he also killed any beneficial insects that may have been ready to pounce, and shocked the beneficial microbes in this soil. Now he has a bigger problem—pesticide-resistant pests. So Bubba is off to the chemical store to pick up the latest flavor that he saw on TV to eradicate the new batch of pests that his old poisons won't kill anymore. And each time his garden is stressed, making the pests the fittest member in Bubba's garden. All along, the pests in your natural garden are lunches and dinners for the good guys.

The natural garden is full of these kinds of reactions. The most active ones go on in the soil where beneficial microbes are competing for space with disease organisms, while some of their compatriots on the good side actually eat the disease organisms. This goes on and on, much to the benefit of the plants growing in this soil. The natural cycle of eat and be eaten is definitely on the side of the natural gardener.

Nature balances things out so that plants will grow to feed other creatures. When I'm in the veggie garden or under the plum tree, I'm very happy about the way the system works.

Predatory Insects

Predators of pest insects have been discussed a few times in this book so far, and this is as good a time as any to cover a few of the more common types that can be seen in natural gardens. We will also be covering some of the pest insects that these predators have an insatiable taste for. Because different people often call insects lots of different names, I'm including the scientific names of each (where necessary) of our beneficial friends in order to minimize confusion. This is not to impress you with my vast knowledge of the insect world, but instead to keep things very clear if you ever choose to order any of these beneficial insects from an insectary to boost the population in your garden.

Aphid Midge (*Aphidoletes Aphidimyza*)

This good guy looks just like a mosquito to many people, and they wonder why mosquitoes would be hovering around an aphid infestation at night. Well, it's the aphid midge, and she means business. The aphid midge will lay her eggs close to an aphid infestation, and in two or three days her rather disgusting-looking larvae hatch. These orange maggots that average about an eighth of an inch in length begin wreaking havoc on the aphid population. They paralyze the aphids with toxic saliva and then suck out their bodily fluids until there is nothing left but a desiccated, mummified aphid. The larvae continue this rampage for about three to five days and then burrow into the soil. In about two weeks, the adult midges emerge from the soil to continue the carnage. Aphid midges will overwinter in the soil, which is another good reason to keep that soil alive. Aphid midges will actively feed on more than 50 different kinds of aphids.

Assassin Bugs (*Reduviidae* family)

This beneficial insect has a very cool name. Kind of like an 007 bug—you know—licensed to kill and all that, old chap. Assassin bugs are somewhat slender bugs that can get as large as half an inch in length. They come in brown and a few other colors, but their most distinguishing feature is an elongated beaklike snout that they skillfully insert into their prey, sucking them dry. Assassin bugs love to eat caterpillars and are considered general predators because of their wide range of prey. Admire these good guys from a distance, as they are known to bite gardeners who like to handle their insect friends. Assassin bugs occur in most gardens, and the best way to keep them in yours is to use no pesticides. They are not very tolerant of chemical toxins and take a long time to recover.

Big-eyed Bugs (*Geocoris* species)

Just as their name so aptly describes them, big-eyed bugs have big eyes. They are fast-moving predators of aphids, spider mites, smaller caterpillars, and leafhoppers. They are considered general predators because of this varied diet. Big-eyed bugs are very common in the western part of North America. Big-eyed bug females lay their eggs on the undersides of leaves in the garden. These insects will over-winter in mulch and in leaf litter. They are voracious pest predators.

Centipedes and Millipedes

Although many people think of them as pests, these two ancient insects actually serve the greater good of the garden and the compost pile. Centipedes feed on insects that inhabit the soil and love to eat mites, as well as the larvae of other soil-dwelling pests, but they will occasionally eat an earthworm. You have to take the good with the bad. Millipedes are voracious eaters of decaying organic matter and are very beneficial to the mulch environment and the compost heap. Controlling these guys is rarely necessary because they are favorite foods of lizards, frogs, and toads.

Damsel Bugs (Nabidae family)

Damsel bugs are rather long and slender bugs that can reach a length of up to a half an inch. They are very fast-moving general predators of aphids, thrips, leafhoppers, and some of the smaller caterpillars. Damsel bugs can often be found around unsprayed alfalfa fields, and using alfalfa as a nitrogen fixer in your garden will draw damsel bugs to the garden. They will overwinter in leaf litter and will be extra happy spending the winter months in a crop of winter alfalfa if your climate permits such plantings. Damsel bugs are very common throughout North America.

Ground Beetles (*Carabidae* family)

Ground beetles are very misunderstood creatures. Everybody thinks they are stinkbugs. They do often strike the same defensive posture, but they are not stinkbugs. Ground beetles are usually iridescent, with a kind of blue-black hue, and they can be brown as well. They are common throughout North America and can reach lengths of up to an inch. Both the adult and the larvae are rather fierce predators of any soil-dwelling pests—including cutworms, root maggots, chafer grubs, and sod webworms; and they have a particular taste for slugs and snails. Some species will actually pursue prey on plants and are known to go after Colorado potato beetle larvae, tent caterpillars, and gypsy moth larvae. They like to hide in leaf litter and under rocks. They are also frequently seen patrolling the natural lawn for bad guys. Bubba would kill them on site.

Hover Flies (*Syrphidae* family)

These beautiful and colorful yellow, or white-and-black-striped, flies can often be seen throughout the natural garden hovering like hummingbirds over flowers that are rich in pollen and nectar. There are several species of hover flies native to all areas of North America. Hover flies lay their eggs, which look kind of like white jars or cylinders among aphid infestations. In a few days (two or three), the eggs hatch and the gray or green larvae (which look a little like a worm or a slug but are actually maggots) begin feeding on the aphid population immediately. The larvae feed on aphids for three to four weeks and then drop to the ground and pupate in your mulch and in the soil. The adults emerge in approximately two weeks, ready to start all over again. Depending on the length of the growing season in your area, you may get up to four generations of hover flies in your garden in a single season.

Lacewings (*Chrysoperla* species)

Lacewings are my favorite general predators in the garden because the adult is so beautiful and benign, and the larvae are right out of a science fiction movie. Lacewing adults are often bright green and sometimes brown—very slender insects with amazingly beautiful gossamer wings and a very distinctive fluttering flight. They have large eyes that are often a metallic gold color, and in some parts are call "goldeneyes."

The adults are pollen and nectar feeders that are particularly fond of the flowers of the carrot family of plants. They lay their eggs close to aphid or other insect infestations on long hairlike follicles, with the egg at the end of the follicle. The larvae hatch from the eggs in less than a week if the weather is warm enough, and then the terror begins. The larvae are shaped like an alligator with a bloated rear end, and are often greenish yellow or a kind of dull tan color. They pursue their prey and then grab their victim in pincerlike jaws and then insert a siphon into the prey and suck the life out of them. Often you can see them actually lifting their prey as they drain them dry.

Lacewing larvae are voracious predators of aphids and have earned the name "Aphid lion" for their exploits. They also love to eat spider mites, mealybugs, soft-scale insects, whiteflies, small caterpillars, and caterpillar eggs, as well as snail and slug eggs. When I see a lacewing larva take an aphid into its jaws prior to cleaning the aphid's clock, I often wonder what kind of horrible sound effect Hollywood could come up with for this display of ferocity. In a good year, you may get three to four generations of lacewings in your garden. The adults and the pupae overwinter in the natural garden.

Lady Beetles (*Coccinellidae* family)

Ladybugs or ladybird beetles are commonly recognized as the most popular of beneficial insects. They are lovely to look at as long as you're looking at the adults; and they serve the natural gardener by eagerly munching on aphids, mealybugs, spider mites, soft-scale insects, and a variety of other bad guys. Some species of lady beetles are rather specialized and will mimic and eat a particular pest exclusively. *Delphastus* lady beetles love to eat whiteflies, while the *Cryptolaemus* lady beetle has a taste for mealybugs and is called The Mealybug Destroyer, not a very dainty name for a lady.

Lady beetle adults are mostly different patterns of black and red or orange. Some are actually yellow, and others have no black spots. Some are black with two red spots (Twice-Stabbed Lady Beetle). The adults mostly feed on nectar and pollen but are known to take a life or two of their favorite pest. The larvae are where the damage is really done to pest populations in the natural garden. Lady beetle larvae are voracious eaters and can consume many times their body weight in pest insects each day. The adults lay their eggs among their favorite food, which is often an aphid infestation. The eggs normally hatch in less than a week, and then the larvae actively hunt prey. The larvae are alligator shaped—normally black with four orange spots on their abdomens.

Lady beetles are often sold to the consumer as a way to control pests. They should not be released during the day! Wait until evening, and release them into a moist garden in the vicinity of the pests. The next morning, many of them will have left, but not before laying a few eggs. So be patient, don't spray anything Bubba might use, and in a few days you'll begin to see larval lady beetles mowing down your pest population. Lady beetles will overwinter as adults in leaf litter.

Minute Pirate Bug (*Orius tristicolor*)

Anything beneficial with the name *pirate* in it has to have a rather ferocious creature. Although the minute pirate bug is rather small in size, it certainly makes up for its size in appetite. These fast-moving

¹/₄-inch-long black and white bugs love to eat thrips, leafhoppers and their nymphs, spider mites, small caterpillars, and a bunch of other smaller pest species. Female minute pirate bugs lay their eggs in plant stems or leaves. The eggs normally hatch in less than a week, and the nymphs actively feed on pests for two to three weeks. You may get as many as four generations of minute pirate bugs in a good season. The adults overwinter in the crevices of tree bark and in leaf litter.

Predatory Mites (*Phytoseiidae* family)

Predatory mites are very small predators of spider mites, citrus red mites, and several other species of pest mites—as well as fungus gnats and some thrips. They are very fast moving and are tan or reddish in color. Females emerge from overwintering in leaf and soil litter and begin laying eggs among their prey when temperatures are warm enough. The eggs hatch in a few days and molt several times until reaching adulthood in about a week and a half. Then the party begins. Predatory mites are very active feeders, and the easiest way to attract them into the garden is not to spray any pesticides, because they are very intolerant of chemical toxins.

Praying Mantid (*Mantis religiosa*)

Praying mantids are widely regarded as garden helpers, with a rather nasty habit of eating their prey (and their mates) head first. They are very active ambushers of all kinds of pest insects but are a bit unselective and will eat just about any bug they can catch, even each other. Protect native mantids by avoiding the use of any pesticides in the garden. These insects are way too valuable to kill with toxic sprays. The eggs of the mantid are glued to the stems of plants and will also overwinter that way, as eggs. Introduced species can really mess up native populations, so refrain from introducing mantids from the store unless you have no natives in your area, or the type you're buying are the native species in your area. Mantids are beautiful creatures, and coming across one in the garden is a rare and unusual treat. I have actually fed them with pest insects laid down in their ambush zone. They are lightning quick and have no table manners.

Rove Beetles (*Staphylinidae* family)

Rove beetles really don't look much like beetles at all. They look more like earwigs, without the pincers on their butts. There are thousands of species of rove beetles native to North America that are active predators of aphids; mites; nematodes; springtails; flies; and some maggots, such as the cabbage maggot and the onion maggot. Rove beetles are also great for your compost pile because they help to decompose organic matter. These beneficial insects overwinter as adults in leaf litter. In the spring, they lay their eggs in the soil, and the larvae actively feed on soil-dwelling pests. Rove beetles love mulch to hide and hunt in.

Soldier Beetles (*Cantharidae* family)

These slender beetles often have orange-colored or red/orange-colored heads and gray wing covers that sometimes have a downy fur on them. These beetles are great predators of corn rootworms, cucumber beetles, grasshopper eggs, aphids, and caterpillars. Female soldier beetles lay their eggs in the soil, and the adults emerge from the soil the following spring. These guys are very helpful for those of you who like to grow corn and squash, so keep an eye out for them. They are fairly common throughout North America.

Spined Soldier Bug (*Podisus maculiventris*)

The spined soldier bug is an important beneficial predator of tent caterpillars, sawfly larvae, Mexican bean beetle larvae, fall army-worms, and a bunch of other caterpillars and grubs. It is a shield-shaped insect with spines on its shoulders, and is normally a brown color with black speckling. Females emerge from overwintering sites in leaf litter and in the soil in spring and begin laying eggs on the leaves of plants close to their prey. The eggs hatch soon after, and the young nymphs may actually feed on plant juices for a little while before succumbing to their voracious appetite for bad guys. Spined soldier beetles are native to North America and are widely found in natural gardens. They are not tolerant of pesticides.

Tiger Beetles (*Cincindelidae* family)

These general predators of pest insects are very colorful and often brightly colored in metallic greens and blues. They are more slender than scarab beetles that we often associate with these metallic colors, but they are just as stupid. The female lays her eggs in burrows of one egg to a hole, and the larvae eat whatever falls in the hole. It's a good thing they don't find tiger beetles at the bottom of abandoned oil wells in Texas. The larvae emerge from the soil as adults and begin hunting for prey. You know that bug zapper in the backyard? Well, these guys are attracted to the light just like moths and other idiots. Considering it takes about three years for a single generation of tiger beetles, you may want to consider putting that zapper away. Tiger beetles are found throughout North America.

Yellow Jackets (*Vespula* species)

I know everybody hates these things at picnics and they're always hovering around your lemonade glass, but yellow jackets are very important predators of other fly species, caterpillars, and whatever else they can carry to the nest. Yellow jackets feed their prey to developing young in the nest. A nest of yellow jackets normally lasts only a single season in one spot. These members of the wasp family will sting you. Yellow jackets can be found near open cans of soda throughout the country!

These are just a few of the many species of beneficial predatory insects that work day in and day out in order to keep the pest populations in your natural garden in check. They are plentiful and will continue to thrive in your garden if you allow their prey to linger on your plants for a little while. As the system improves in your garden, you will see faster and faster response times by the beneficial predatory and parasitic insects, and soon you'll be drinking a glass of lemonade (and fighting off yellow jackets) while old Gardenzilla, I mean Bubba, is still spraying away with the latest poisons. Along with the predatory beneficial insects, there are several native species of pest parasites as well. We will touch on a few of them in this next section.

Parasitic Beneficial Insects

If you thought that the way some of the predatory beneficial insects went about their daily search for food was brutal, you should get a load of our next group of good guys. Parasitic beneficial insects have the market cornered on efficiency and on the merciless treatment of pests. Nature is a cruel and brutal place when you think about lions and tiger and bears. But when it comes to pest control, I kind of like the efficiency of the system. I like the fact that nature reacts with precision when an imbalance occurs. Unfortunately for the squeamish, this precision is often a little bit distasteful. So if you're squeamish and a little grossed out by the whole reality of the way nature does her thing, think of old Bubba and the Soylent Green on his lawn and in his garden. Think about how he's damaging the environment that all of us get to live in, and think about the immediate environment his children are growing up in. Now that's gross. Compared to Gardenzilla, a few parasites that feed on the pests in your natural garden are quite tame.

Braconid Wasps (*Braconidae* family)

These tiny wasps that do not exceed a half an inch in length are very efficient parasites of a multitude of pests. Braconids are too busy and too small to give the gardener any attention, so do not fear the braconid wasp. Her name is scarier than she is unless you're an aphid, codling moth larvae, an elm bark beetle, a hornworm, an armyworm, a cabbageworm, or any of a bunch of other pests. The braconid is something to truly fear if you're one of these guys. Braconids are sometimes only a tenth of an inch long; they have a threadlike waist, and are normally brown or black. Female braconids inject their eggs into the host one at a time or in large numbers. The larvae of the braconid then develop inside the host. When they are finished with their development, they spin cocoons near to or right on the dead host. Then they pupate, and the adults emerge from the cocoons in only a few days, depending on the species and how warm the weather is.

If you have ever seen a dead tomato hornworm on or near your tomato plants that has what looks like a bunch of little white eggs on its back, you can thank a braconid wasp for removing that pest from your tomatoes. Braconids are native to North America and can be lured into your garden by planting lots of flowers that are rich in nectar and pollen. The adults are nectar and pollen feeders and are especially fond of the flowers produced by members of the carrot family of plants such as dill, parsley, celery, carrots, and fennel. All of these plants are useful for other purposes as well. These types of plants are sometimes referred to as "companion plants" and will be discussed a little later on.

Ichneumon Wasps *(Ichneumonidae* family*)*

The members of the ichneumon wasp family are also very efficient parasites of a number of caterpillars. They also like some beetle larvae and sawfly maggots. Ichneumon wasps can range in size from a tenth of an inch to over an inch in length. Some species have very long, needle-thin ovipositors, which can get three inches long and are often mistaken for stingers by gardeners, found running and screaming from the garden. The ichneumon wasp is a benevolent creature with way too much work to do than to bother antagonizing a creature that looks more like a tree to it than a gardener. They're in your garden to clean up the caterpillars, and that's all they're thinking about. Ichneumon females lay their eggs inside of a host pest through that long ovipositor. The larvae then develop inside the host, often emerging from the host as adults. Ichneumon wasps are very important to the natural gardener and can be the difference between a ravaged crop of pears and one that is just right. The beneficial parasites can sometime produce eight to ten generations in a single growing season. Next time you see one, fear not; this insect is a friend of the highest order.

These two parasites of pests are very capable and will work wonders in your garden. The adults really appreciate it when you let a few of your vegetable or culinary herbs go to flower, and they will reward you with sentinel-like controls of some of the bad guys that periodically plague the garden. No discussion of beneficial insects is complete without saying how important it is that you encourage honeybee and bees of any kind in the natural garden. These busy creatures have one job to do for you, and that is pollination. These tireless workers pollinate our fruit trees and our vegetables. Using pesticides hurts them and reduces their numbers, which in turn reduces flower pollination in the garden, which reduces fruit and vegetable production. In the natural garden, everything is linked, and the chain is fragile in the beginning. After just a single season of pesticide-free gardening, you'll see huge changes in the amount of life buzzing around the garden tending to their business. It is a miracle, and bees are a big part of it.

Before we go on, there are two non-insect beneficial organisms that should be mentioned. Decollate snails are predatory snails that hunt and eat the brown garden snail. It should be noted that they will eat tender plants if there are no brown garden snails around to eat. Parasitic nematodes are some very beneficial organisms that fight bad guys above and below the soil. They enter the host and infect it with an intestinal toxin that stops many pests and pest species of nematodes from populating your garden.

All said, the beneficial insects that you draw and harbor in your natural garden will work without rest to maintain balance. It's a good thing to have a few pests around so that you can keep the beneficial guys on the job. Share a little bit of the garden with some pests, and watch how nature works her magic.

Soil Pests

Pests that *inhabit* the soil can be just as numerous and destructive to plants as those *above* the soil level. The only problem is that often we have no idea what they're doing to our plants until it's too late. In a living soil, however, there are thousands of checks and balances to stem the tide of insect pests, and there are several practices that the natural gardener can perform to assist. One of the most common cultural practices used by the natural gardener to deter pest populations from getting out of hand in the soil is to rotate plantings of some of their more vulnerable crops to different spots in the garden each year. Specific pests such as onion maggots or carrot maggots will not attack certain other plants. It is a good idea to use the practice of crop rotation on your more mobile plants such as vegetables and annual flowers in order to interrupt the plans a particular pest may have for staying in your garden.

For instance, if your tomatoes and carrots are being overrun with nematode problems, you can plant African marigolds in the area. These beautiful flowers emit toxins to the nematodes, and they won't be a problem any longer. If they do return, isn't it a bummer—all you have to do is plant more marigolds. It is also wise to keep in mind that your living soil harbors many organisms that find these soil dwelling pests a tasty treat. I'm also a big believer in the chicken tractor. If I have a pest such as the plum curculio beetle bothering my fruit trees, I build a chicken enclosure around the tree, extending a few feet past the dripline. Then I turn a few chickens loose in the enclosure. In very short order, I no longer have a pest problem, and the chickens fertilized my trees as they were working. Some of you may not have a desire to have chickens, but rove beetles and spined soldier bugs love curculios, and they live in the mulch under the tree already. Soil-dwelling pests are no problem for the natural gardener. As a matter of fact, a few of those rascals actually helps to keep the good guys at home.

Disease Control and How the Soil Biology Works

The living soil cultivated by natural gardeners by adding load after load of compost and mulch to the soil while maintaining a good mineral and nutrient balance is one of the best ways to prevent and suppress disease-causing organisms from taking hold in the garden. The beneficial microorganisms that live in your soil work on disease organisms by either eating them or by suppressing them with "competitive exclusion." This battle tactic on a microscopic scale is very effective at keeping the bad organisms at bay.

If a disease organism affects and takes hold on a plant in this living soil, the beneficial organisms often build a ring around the infected area surrounding the disease-infected soil, with organisms that feed on the disease or suppress it so it cannot spread. Plant losses do occur on occasion, but epidemic infections are very rare and are usually due to some imbalance somewhere in the soil. The gradual improvement of the soil with further doses of organic matter along with careful monitoring of the minerals in the soil can keep your garden fighting disease until you no longer tend the garden. When and if plants do expire from a disease infection, it is a good idea to remove them from the garden completely and send them to the greenwaste facility where they hot-compost the disease away, or incinerate the plant and use the ash back in the soil. If you keep the biological engine running, the engine will keep running. There is no easier way to say it.

Integrated Pest Management (IPM)

IPM is an abbreviation for Integrated Pest Management. For conventional agriculture still mired in the dependency on chemical pesticides, this means that nature has found a way to help reduce the use of rescue chemistry every time a farmer sees a bug he or she doesn't like. Insect breeders have developed predatory and parasitic beneficial insects that have a resistance to certain pesticides. And while it doesn't seem like a very sound practice to release bugs into a cropping system resistant to toxins, it does actually make some sense.

Farmers are using more and more powerful and toxic substances to control pests. If you're introducing a predator into a population of pest insects that is resistant to the insecticides used to control the pests, there is a possibility that the predatory species may actually take hold in this environment and help the farmer reduce his or her dependency on the chemicals. If pest populations are higher than acceptable, the insecticide is used in lower concentrations or as spot treatments, instead of bombing the whole crop. Another way in which IPM is used is to select botanical or less powerful insecticides that are not harmful to the beneficial insects and are somewhat effective on the target pest species. This may not seem like a good thing, but it really is. Any small steps that are taken and accepted as good practice that are less toxic to our food supply and to our environment are good steps. We, on the other side, have to be just as patient with the chemical users as we are with nature. They're slowly coming to realize that natural and organic growers are not a bunch of tree-hugging space cadets. We understand something about nature that they lost somewhere. Patience is truly a virtue; they'll come to their senses.

Companion Plantings

Companion plants are a very fun and interesting way to gain an even greater understanding of how the natural system and the practice of natural gardening works. There are certain plants that have an effect on other plants, disease organisms, and insects. These plants are often ornamentals, herbs, or vegetables that you may already be growing in your garden, but don't know what they are doing to protect your personal Eden. We could spend another whole book on this subject and not even begin to touch on the dynamics of species interaction. Suffice it to say that there are some very common garden-variety (pun intended) plants that lure beneficial insects to your garden because their pollen and nectar are irresistible. There are other plants that chase and repel pests, and there are some plants that are just downright toxic to pest insects and disease organisms. When these plants are used in the garden for their specific talents and characteristics, they become companions to the gardener and the garden. I also refer to the plants that take nitrogen from the atmosphere and fix it into the soil as some of my companions; however, conventional wisdom refers to them as *green manures* or *legumes* when speaking of the nitrogen fixers in the pea family of plants. They're our companions now. Let's take a quick look at some of them.

Nitrogen-Fixing Plants

Alfalfa, buckwheat (not Spanky's pal), clover, beans, and peas are just a few of the plants that take nitrogen out of the air and fix it into the soil through a complex but simple relationship with soil-dwelling parasitic beneficial bacteria, of which the most common type is known as *Rhizobium* bacteria.

Plants That Lure Beneficial Insects

This category includes all of the above plants, with the addition of carrots, parsley, anise, fennel, celery, dill, the entire mint family, some members of the chrysanthemum family, and a whole bunch of weeds. Many of my natural gardening friends actually cultivate small weed patches around the garden, and mix in a few ornamentals to disguise the weeds in order to keep their beneficial insect populations at home.

Plants That Repel Pests and Are Toxic to Them

The entire onion clan, including the entire garlic species, is very good at chasing certain pests from the garden. Many people plant them close to their roses and tomatoes for this purpose. The African marigold is a very important plant for nematode controls.

Companion plants are much more numerous than this tiny sampling, and I strongly suggest that if you're inclined to do some research on your own that you endeavor to understand species interactions a bit more. You'll find it a very interesting topic for discovery. Nature figured out how to make these plants interact with insects, diseases, and the air. It is in our best interest as natural gardeners or chemical users to see if any of these plants can benefit our gardens.

The Efficiency of the System

In this chapter and in this book, I have attempted to show the cyclical nature of all things in the garden. I have tried to make the most complex biological processes seem rather elementary. I have done this not to patronize, but to make the incredible miracle of nature seem a little easier and friendlier. (Major concepts such as nature, the national debt, and the roller derby are difficult to grasp from the perspective of a single human being. Okay, the national debt is pretty straightforward, but that roller derby just confuses me. How do they score points when it appears they spend most of their time beating the _____ out of each other? Oh, yeah, this is a gardening book.)

Nature is big and very complex, so if after reading this book you feel like you can walk out into your garden and understand how the whole thing works a little better, I have done my job. And if after reading this book you are now inclined to try natural gardening practices on your own property, my work is just beginning.

This book is a companion to my first book, *Natural Gardening A–Z*. If you pick up that book, you will see some of the topics we have discussed in the form of an A–Z list. *Natural Gardening A–Z* will provide you with a quick reference to specific pest controls, and will complement this book in the garden.

I hope that you feel closer to the world outside, and that this book helped you get there without too much new vocabulary and in an easy-to-understand quick way. *The Complete Natural Gardener* was meant to increase your understanding of the soil and how it affects every aspect of the garden, along with an increased understanding of gardening techniques without making them sound like VCR programming instructions. The natural garden is an ecosystem on a very small scale, but we natural gardeners strive to make it a complete ecosystem on that very small scale. I now send you out into the world to buy as much cow poop as you can afford. Thank you for your time and attention.

Afterword

Natural gardeners are very unique and special people. They (you and I) have chosen to make an attempt to harness the incredible forces of nature and put those forces to work on a reduced scale. I like to think that we do this because of a higher purpose, but in my case, it always goes back to the fact that I just don't like to work too much. I do like letting nature take a large portion of my gardening chores to make her own. Yes, I'm a lazy gardener. And while natural gardens are no less stunning than the sterile chemical kind, I like to wander in my garden more than spray or feed or worry. I like to watch that lacewing larva going on its merry way looking for new aphid populations to terrorize. I like the idea of saving money on watering the garden because the soil in a natural garden holds on to moisture better than the sterile garden. I also like to sit with a glass of lemonade shooing away yellow jackets while the birds sing and lizards scurry around in their endless search for food.

I like the hawks and the owls, and I understand that the rabbits and mice they eat from the garden are their natural food. I know that since those rodents are feeding on my plants, the raptors won't have to deal with toxins once they catch their lunch. I like the fact that the soil in a natural garden is a filter and a storehouse of power at the same time. To me, the reason for gardening naturally is simple—I like nature, and I like having nature around me. So I do it this way.

A Statement in Favor of the Environment

I am very much against alarmism—I don't like it when environmentalists do destructive things to draw attention to their plight. I think that taking one's own space and doing what one can to ensure that little or no environmental impact originates from that space is the highest form of environmental activism. If I were to splash red paint all over your white car, you would probably be angry with me. Well, I think of toxic runoff and chemical garden materials as red paint. And I am not about to splash your environment with toxic stuff from my paint can (property). I'm sure that your children like to go to the beach or to the lake and swim. What right do I have to splash red paint there? None. I have no right to impact the environment you inhabit. So I do my best not to.

A natural garden prevents red paint from being splashed all over the place. Yes, it's very easy to get angry with Bubba because of his disregard for the environment, but wouldn't it be more productive to show old Bubba a few of your tricks and see what he thinks? You may convert an ignorant gorilla into the club. And if he laughs at your seemingly simplistic approach to what he figures is only something a petrochemical giant understands, show him your tomatoes or your roses. He may not let on, but it will make that oxygen-deprived brain creak a little.

Enough Bubba bashing. The natural gardener is on the front lines of an environmental revolution championed by a woman or a man and their compost heap. I kind of like the sound of that.

The Sensibility of Natural Gardening

Well, if we haven't already figured out the sensibility of natural gardening by now, what the heck are we doing here? Gardening in partnership with the greatest force on the planet has to make some sense. Instead of fighting nature, we accept and tweak her a little. Instead of throwing our hands up in defeat because the bugs didn't die the last time we carpet-bombed the garden, natural gardeners thank the lady beetle for her voracious appetite. Instead of ripping out a whole bed of petunias because we burned them with what three gentlemen gardeners said made their petunias thrive, natural gardeners appreciate the subtlety of compost. I guess that the simple approach really is a more sensible way. Simple works for me, and I hope that a greater understanding of the natural garden helps your gardening projects get simpler, too.

Teaching our Children about the Natural World

One of the most important things an adult can do is teach their children what they know. When it comes to giving them some input on how nature works, kids just eat it up. Their natural inquisitiveness comes flying out of them with a multitude of whys and hows. They observe the things you show them and then gladly give you their unsolicited opinions on how things *really work*. I have seen children engrossed for hours in the workings of nature when some of those details are shown to them. Then they come up with either the most simple and astute assumptions or the most hilarious observations you ever heard. Whether it is one or the other, one thing is for certain: They're using their minds.

A child I once knew who is now a young man (and who happens to be my nephew Brandon) used to be fascinated by snails. Brandon would observe their every move as if it were some detailed scientific study. To him, it was more than that; it was nature in her finest moment as a snail. He would share his insights on snails with his parents (my sister and brother-in-law) at great length and with excruciating thoroughness. These observations and the conclusions Brandon came up with were incredible in their detail and completely out-of-control funny. Brandon made his conclusion after he had observed snails for many an hour. When his experiment was complete, his work was done in the finest spirit of science. Who cares if he was right or not—that little boy was using his brain. I don't know if he ate any of the snails in order to arrive at his final verdict on snails and nature as seen through the eyes of a two-year-old, but he made a strong position.

My niece Meghan used to love the San Diego Zoological Society's

Wild Animal Park. I'm not sure if she still does. But one time when my mother had escorted both of her grandchildren to the park, Meghan announced when the train that runs through the park stopped in a particularly ripe area, "Mimi [her name for her grand-mother], it smells like nature." How could a clearer and more perfectly simple observation ever be made? When my mom told me about Meghan's assessment of how nature smells, I laughed and laughed. And then I realized that she was absolutely correct—the odor that was wafting through the air certainly "smelled like nature." To Meghan, nature smelled like camel dung or something similar that day among the residents of the park.

I have recently met a little miracle named Ava Frances Tracy. I hope that she will get an opportunity to inform her mother and father about how snails work or how nature smells on a certain day. Today, Ava's job is to drive her mother and father into sleepless delirium. But soon I hope she will be out observing the intoxicating fragrance of a gardenia in her garden and witness her mom's horse use the toilet. What kind of conclusions do you think a child will make with those two sensory images?

The moral of this story is that our children deserve to see how we see the natural world—if only to tell us how wrong we are when we tell them that chickens come from eggs. It is our duty to get them out from in front of the television set or the Nintendo machine and out into a world where smell, touch, and perception are used as much as their sense of sight. Gardens are also great places for our children to play with us. Games like hide-and-go-seek in the vegetable garden will draw them to the bean tipis. Showing them where the lettuce comes from and allowing them to debate the subject puts their devel-oping minds in gear. Playing on the lawn can turn into scientific observations of the most ridiculous fashion, and the lawn itself becomes a source of curiosity and thought.

I really think that if we asked Mother Nature, she would tell us to teach our children everything we know about Her. And then let our children tell us what they think. Thinking—I imagine that that's exactly what nature intended.

A Mission for the Future

Louise L. Hay, a dear friend, a passionate natural gardener, and the publisher of this book, recently asked me to contribute to a work she compiled of thoughts for the next generation of our species. The book is called *Millennium 2000: A Positive Approach* (Hay House, 1999). Louise was tired of all of the alarmism about the change of millennia, and how much really weird stuff is coming out of the fatalistic rhetoric from self-appointed authorities on the future. So she assembled a group of very smart people (and me) so we could present our thoughts about the great things that are in store for our collective lives as time marches on. This was my humble contribution:

Earthkeeping: A Word for the New Millennium

Hello, fellow Earthlings, and welcome to the new millennium party. As we all embark on this journey into the 21st century, I'd like to speak to you about a word I thought up recently: *Earthkeeping*. It may take the rest of my life to fully grasp the meaning of this newly formed noun, but it certainly is a word for the new millennium

We human beings have our work cut out for us in so many ways as we form the clay that will be our legacy for the generations to follow. While this evolution takes place, we must not forget that no matter how advanced our technologies become, nature and the natural world will never be obsolete. This planet has been our home, and we will be asked to be better Earthkeepers if we intend it to be our home in the future. As our technologies grow in spirit, the one constant will be Earth. While we are making affirmations about love, personal growth, love, spiritual awareness, love, responsibilities, and more love, shouldn't the environment that sustains us also be included in this mantra?

Take a moment and think about some of the most incredible and breathtaking things that you have witnessed in your life. Is nature or some natural wonder in there somewhere?

We are fed, clothed, and sheltered by this amazing orb spinning through space. Earth is such a precious and unique phenomenon, and we are so very fortunate to inhabit such a place. I wonder if we sometimes forget how rare and extraordinary we humans are. We are capable of such deep feelings and so much loveliness. This is all made possible by our Earth and the nature we call Mother. As we hurry along in order to pay our bills, raise our children, and grow into better people, Earth waits patiently for us to partake in her beauty and her bounty.

In the coming century, let us endeavor to understand and appreciate our planet so that we may better comprehend the new worlds we are destined to encounter as we look to the stars. To gain this knowledge of our planet, we must develop respect for the fantastic diversity of living organisms that inhabit her, along with us. With this respect, together we can heal what we have damaged and nurture Mother Earth, who has nurtured *us* for so long.

Earthkeeping—a word for the next millennium.

I'll see you in the Garden!

— Don

Resources

RECOMMENDED READING

Books

- Gershuny, Grace and Joseph Smillie. *The Soul of the Soil: A Guide to Ecological Soil Management.* Second Edition, St. Johnsbury, Vt.: GAIA Services, 1986.

- Cox, Jeff. *Landscaping with Nature.* Emmaus, Pa.: Rodale Press, 1991.

- Creasy, Rosalind. *The Complete Book of Edible Landscaping.* San Francisco, Ca.: Sierra Club Books, 1982.

- Martin, Deborah L., and Grace Gershuny, eds. *The Rodale Book of Composting.* Emmaus, Pa.: Rodale Press, 1992.

- Stebbins, Robert L., and Michael MacCaskey. *Pruning: How-To Guide for Gardeners.* Los Angeles, Ca.: HP Books, 1983.

- Schulz, Warren. *The Chemical-Free Lawn: The Newest Varieties and Techniques to Grow Lush, Hardy Grass.* Emmaus, Pa.: Rodale Press, 1989.

Periodicals

- *Common Sense Pest Control Quarterly,* Bio-Integral Resource Center (BIRC), P.O. Box 7414, Berkeley, CA 94707.

- *The IPM Practitioner,* Bio-Integral Resource Center (BIRC), P.O. Box 7414, Berkeley, CA 94707.

- *Country Living's Gardener,* Hearst Communications, Inc., 1790 Broadway, 12th floor, New York, NY 10019.

- *Rebecca's Garden,* Hearst Communications, Inc., 1790 Broadway, 12th floor, New York, NY 10019.

- *Organic Gardening,* Rodale Press, Inc., 33 East Minor Street, Emmaus, PA 18098.

Gardening Products

Supplies

- Environmental Health Science, Corp., Producers of natural fertilizers and Kelzyme fossilized kelp soil conditioners. P.O. Box 548, Provo, UT 84603, 295 Neptune Avenue, Encinitas, CA 92024

- Gardener's Supply Company, 128 Intervale Road, Burlington VT 05401

- Gardens Alive!, 5100 Schenley Place, Lawrenceburg, IN 47025

- Peaceful Valley Farm Supply, P.O. Box 2209, Grass Valley, CA 95945

General Gardening Seeds and Goodies

• W. Atlee Burpee and Company, 300 Park Avenue, Warminster, PA 18974

• Henry Field's Seed and Nursery Company, 415 North Burnett Street, Shenandoah, IA 51602

• Gurney Seed and Nursery Company, 110 Capital Street, Yankton, SD 57078

• Hasting's Seeds, P.O. Box 115535, Atlanta, GA 30310-8535

• Park Seed Company, P.O. Box 31, Greenwood, SC 29647

• Pinetree Garden Seed, Route 100, New Gloucester, ME 04260

Vegetable Seeds

• Bountiful Gardens, 18001 Shafer Ranch Road, Willits, CA 95490
    Untreated seeds for vegetables, grains, herbs, and flowers. Books and gardening supplies.

• The Cook's Garden, P.O. Box 535, Londonderry, VT 05148
    Herb and vegetable seeds for the serious kitchen garden. Many gourmet seed selections from Italy and France.

• Garden City Seeds, 778 Highway 93 North, Hamilton, MT 59840
    Specializing in vegetables and flowers for the northern gardener.

• The Gourmet Gardener, 8650 College Boulevard, Dept. 205SJ, Overland Park, KS 66210
    Herb, vegetable, and edible flower seeds from all over the world.

- Heirloom Garden Seeds, P.O. Box 138, Guerneville, CA 95446
  Seeds of very old varieties of vegetables, herbs, and more.

- Johnny's Selected Seeds, 310 Foss Hill Road, Albion, ME 04910
  Lots of choices, including some very unusual vegetables.

- Seeds of Change, P.O. Box 15700, Santa Fe, NM 87505
  Many heirloom and traditional native vegetables, as well as a unique selection of flowers and medicinal/culinary herbs.

- Tomato Growers Supply Company, P.O. Box 2237,
  Fort Myers, FL 33902
  More than 250 varieties of tomatoes for those of you who just can't get enough.

Herb Seeds

- Companion Plants, 7247 North Coolville Ridge Road,
  Athens, OH 45701
  Really neat selection of rare and unusual herbs for the kitchen and to draw beneficial insects to the garden.

- Nichol's Garden Nursery, 1190 North Pacific Highway,
  Albany, OR 45701
  One of the best selections of medicinal and culinary herbs.

- Richter's, 357 Highway 47, Goodwood, Ontario, Canada L0C 1A0
  An amazing selection of herbs.

Fruits

- Country Heritage Nursery, P.O. Box 536, Hartford, MI 49057
  Fruit and nut trees—a very nice selection.

- Edible Landscaping, P.O. Box 77, Afton, VA 22920
  Interesting ideas for fruits and nuts in the residential garden.

- Northwoods Nursery, 27635 South Oglesby Road,
  Canby, OR 97013
  Fruits of all kinds.

- Raintree Nursery, 391 Butts Road, Morton, WA 98356
  Hundreds of edible plants from all over the world, including fruits, nuts, and berries of all kinds. Specializes in disease-resistant varieties for the home gardener.

- St. Lawrence Nurseries, R.R. 5, Box 324, Potsdam, NY 13676
  A wide variety of fruits and nuts for the eastern gardener.

- Stark Brother's Nursery, P.O. Box 10, Louisiana, MO 63353
  An old nursery with a long history of quality plants. A very good selection of fruits and nuts for almost every climate.

Flowers

- Kurt Bluemel, Inc., 2740 Greene Lane, Baldwin, MD 21013
  Good selection of eastern favorites.

- Buena Creek Gardens, 418 Buena Creek Road,
  San Marcos, CA 92067
  A wide selection of perennials specializing in hybrid daylilies.

- Canyon Creek Nursery, 3527 Dry Creek Road, Oroville, CA 95965
  Uncommon perennials and a good selection of hardy geraniums.

- A High Country Garden, 2902 Rufina Street, Santa Fe, NM 87505
  Hardy and water-thrifty perennials, and interesting rock garden selections.

- Milaeger's Gardens, 4838 Douglas Avenue, Racine, WI 53402
  Wide selection of hardy perennials.

- Wayside Gardens, 1 Garden Lane, Hodges, SC 29695
  One of the premier catalog nurseries in the world.

- White Flower Farm, Litchfield, CT 06759
  Great selection of perennials for all eastern climates.

Bulbs

- A and D Peony and Perennial Nursery, 6808 180th, SE, Snohomish, WA 98290
  Peonies and a wide selection of other bulbs.

- Aitken's Salmon Creek Garden, 608 NW 119th Street, Vancouver, WA 98685
  Irises of all kinds, bearded and beardless.

- B and D Lilies, 330 P Street, Port Townsend, WA 98368
  Asiatic and Oriental hybrids, trumpets, and species lilies.

- Dutch Gardens, P.O. Box 200, Adelphia, NJ 07710
  Bulbs of all kinds for spring and summer bloom.

- Van Bourgondien Brothers, Box 1000, 245 Farmingdale Road, Route 109, Babylon, NY 11702
  World-renowned nursery, and producers of a wide selection of bulbs.

About the Author

Donald W. Trotter, Ph.D., is a naturalist and environmental scientist. He grew up in a family where commercial farming was a part of daily life. Don pursued the love of plants shown to him by his family, and went ahead with his education in finding out how to preserve the fragile balance of nature in farming as well as in the residential garden. From the farm to the front yard, it is Don's belief that no one needs to use harmful chemicals in order to successfully tend to one's garden. He is also the author of *Natural Gardening A–Z*.

We hope you enjoyed this Hay House book.
If you would like to receive a free catalog featuring additional
Hay House books and products, or if you would like information
about the Hay Foundation, please contact:

Hay House, Inc.
P.O. Box 5100
Carlsbad, CA 92018-5100

(760) 431-7695 or **(800) 654-5126**
(760) 431-6948 (fax) or **(800) 650-5115 (fax)**

Please visit the Hay House Website at: **www.hayhouse.com**